Smile Big, Run Hard

50 Miles Every day for 50 Days

by

Sam Boatwright

Grosvenor House
Publishing Limited

This book is published by
Grosvenor House Publishing Ltd
28-30 High Street, Guildford, Surrey, GU1 3EL.
www.grosvenorhousepublishing.co.uk

A CIP record for this book
is available from the British Library

ISBN 978-1-78148-211-7

To Mum and Dad.

Thank you.

You made me the man that made it round.

Contents

Prologue

Before I even tell you about my stupidly long run, I need to make sure that I thank a lot of different people as there were so many people that got me to the finish line. I got all the plaudits for the run, but without the support I received, I would have never have made it. I couldn't decide the best way to do this, as there were so many people that went in to making this happen, so I thought a big list would be the best way! So here goes.

A massive thank you goes to: Mum, Dad, Trev Boatwright, Luke Boatwright, Sara Wellock, Harriet Boatwright, Uncle Ian, Aunty Glen, Emily, Brian and Kath Wellock, Ian and Dianne Wellock, James Wellock, Jane Peggs, Tom Mayfield, Matty Wilson, Matthew Speres, Jonathan Richards, Tony Phoenix-Morrison, Kate Dinsdale, Sam Stonnell, Gayle Sharp, Jo Kenny, Kev Green, Rachel Capstick, Paddy Capstick, Skipton RFC, North Ribblesdale RUFC, Andy Jackson, Nick Magooligan, Julie Beck, Kirstie Ingham, Chris Sharp, Paul Lacy, Shaun Barraclough, Matthew Hosier, Gary Mayfield, Alex Rogers, Robin Hargreaves, Christa Baldwin, Amanda Robinson, Louisa Titorenko, Neil Foster, all the local Primary Schools, Marcus Peel (Malsis), Andrew Rex, Jan Michaels, Phillip Green, Theresa Slater, Adam Oldfield, Mark McGlinchey,

Alison McGlinchey, Liz Leighton, Kev Greaves, Chris Carniss and Helen Carniss.

There are so many people to thank and I have no doubt forgotten someone. If I have missed you off this list, I am sorry; your support was no less appreciated. You all made the run a great success and we all contributed to a great cause. Out of this list, I must single out the Wellock family. Every single one of you has my gratitude and I might never have said it enough, but thank you – without your contributions, the run would never have reached the start line.

Smile Big, Run Hard by Sam Boatwright:
50 Miles Every day for 50 Days.

Epic Run.

CHAPTER 1

Why Run?

Sunday 27th May, 2011.

"Hey Mate," I said down the phone which was fairly usual after a Saturday night in town. This phrase usually carried with it the questions of, "How are you? How pissed did you get last night? Are you alone? And what are you up to today?" The reply, as usual, was:

"Yeah, Bru, I'm alright. We out today?" I should probably have mentioned that Matt is South African, hence, the 'Bru'.

"I fancy doing something stupid pal, something that we have never done, but will remember, and something that will push our bodies and minds to the absolute limit." I could tell by the silence that Matt's mind was working overtime. Not only was he hung over, I was not.

"You want to meet at the Castle about 2, Bru?" He finally replied through a gravelled voice. Matt's reply suggested he had not really understood what the hell I was talking about. The Castle is a local pub, often frequented after a tough rugby game or on a Sunday afternoon when the sun is out. The pub, like its namesake, stands at the top of Skipton's High Street and is great for people-watching on a lazy summer's day. Unfortunately for Matt on this summer's day, the pub was not what I was planning.

"I am 30 next year mate," I began, though not too sure Matt knew what the hell was going on.

"I want to do something hard. Something that might push us so hard we might not be able to take it. Maybe Everest?... Or Kilamanjaro... Actually, scrap that. Chris Moyles got up Kilamanjaro and if he can do that, I don't think it will push us hard enough. Everest would be good, but I think even that might be expensive." The conversation was very one sided. So much so, that I was answering my own questions, not even sure if Matt was still awake on the other end. I was reasonably confident that whatever my suggestion, he would go along with it, if for nothing else than to just get me off the phone so he could continue with his hangover. There are a number of other reasons why I would choose not to go up Everest:

1. I am scared of heights
2. I don't like camping
3. I have never been climbing
4. I don't like been cold
5. I moan….a lot!

"I know!" I said in an almost cartoon, light-bulb-above-the-head idea kind of moment. "We can run!" Enthusiasm and excitement was pouring out of me now.

"We can run – around the UK. I have just read a book about some woman who ran round the world, so the UK can't be that hard?! Yeah…. I could run a bit and then you could run a bit? ….Like a relay???!!!" The idea was placed. I was full of ideas.

Like many of you that know me already, I am very good at ideas, but the actual planning and execution is something else entirely! This was going to need a lot of planning and preparation. Although at this moment in time, I really didn't care; that was not what I was thinking about. I was thinking about all the amazing things we would see and the unbelievable achievement our bodies would feel when we had finished. I thought nothing about the pain the run would cause me, or about the finance it would take just to get the idea off the ground.

CHAPTER 2

Me

Sailor, Pot Washer, Waiter, Ice-Cream Salesman, Market Stall Owner, Barman, Telesales, Gym Instructor, Fitness Instructor, Marketeer, Salesman, Employment Coach, Slaughter House Knifeman, Warehouse Operative, Shelf Stacker, Teacher, Fruit Picker, Cleaner, Builder, Electrician, Joiner, Painter, Driver, Personal Trainer..... Ultra-Marathoner and Writer? Why not?

I am 29 years old and I guess from the jobs listed above, you might call me a quitter. I don't really class myself as a quitter, rather I have just never really found anything that I like doing. I love staying in shape and pushing my body to the limit. This has been the same since I was young. The jobs listed are not really in any order, although the last three are my most recent. I always wanted to be a writer, but as an ex-girlfriend's Dad once put it, "You have the imagination of a potato!" So, writing a fictional novel was never going to be my forte. The only part of a novel I could get to was, 'Once upon a time', or 'In a galaxy far, far away', and I am fairly positive these have been used before. My only option left for writing was to write about something real, something that I had done. I have travelled quite a lot and I have seen different countries and experienced new cultures, but throughout my teens and twenties, I might have been classed as a yob. I was your typical Brit! I went to places to see how drunk I could get within the first three hours of stepping off the plane, and so a book about being drunk in Australia, America and Europe, with the odd game of rugby thrown in, probably wouldn't appeal to most people.

Even during these years of what you might call 'excess', I was still always wondering how much my body would take. This was why I was the one that at the end of the night that was a dribbling wreck; I am the one you didn't want to invite to your wedding, but always came as someone's plus one. I was as Peter Kay might put it, 'Uncle Knobhead'.

I grew up in a tiny village in the Yorkshire Dales called Malham. Growing up in Malham is hard – not hard like growing up in the ghetto or some poverty stricken third world country; it is hard because you are so isolated. Everyone in the Dales works hard for what they get, whether they work the land or they rely on hospitality and tourism. My Dad worked in the family business – a beautiful country guest house called Beck Hall. It sat right on the bank of the River Aire and my brothers, cousins and I spent most summer afternoons playing in canoes on the river. Once we were old enough, we worked for the family business. Like I said, everyone in the Dales works. It's this work ethic that pushes me now, through the pain barrier. Never stopping.

I remember when I was about 15, I had just started playing senior rugby; I was crapping myself. Massive, grizzly blokes, many of whom were ex-first team players on their way down the teams, still looking for a victim to smash into on a Saturday afternoon. My Dad turned to me, as I was picking myself up from what must have been the 200th time someone had smashed into me, and said, "No matter how much it hurts, no matter how many times they knock you down, you get back up, smile, and smash back." It was not advice that I stuck to right away, but whilst I was running, whilst my body was screaming, his voice echoed in my mind.

High School was not my most productive time. I knew what I wanted to do and school was not it. I had always wanted to join the forces. Having visited the Armed Forces Careers Office, I decided that the Royal Navy was the life I wanted. As it happened, the country kid was not ready for the expanses of the sea and I was soon back at home, although by this time, Foot and Mouth had hit the Yorkshire Dales and my parents had moved down the road to the small town of Skipton. I returned to the Dales without much of a clue about what to do. One thing the Navy did do – it made a man out of the kid that went away. I am sure any serviceman or woman would tell you, it makes you self-dependant, confident in your abilities (whatever they might be) and it helps you to focus. Once I knew what my goals were, I set about achieving them. Many of the jobs that I have had were short-lived due to circumstances. I needed money for college, a car or university. Unfortunately, even after university, I still had no idea what I wanted to do. I love working with people and most of the jobs that I had were people orientated. Most of all, I love to inspire others, whether that is my team on the rugby field, a child in a classroom, or a client in the gym. If I can inspire anyone to do something to make their lives better, I would argue that there is no better feeling in the world. I think that's why I chose to run.

CHAPTER 3

So you want to be an Endurance Athlete?

What did I know about marathon running? Well, nothing, to be brutally honest. 26.2 miles of pretty pointless running! At least when you are playing rugby, you are running to score or running because if you don't, some fat, giant ape will land on you!! When playing rugby, it is always to win, to beat the opposition. Running distances always just seemed so long and boring; by the time you have finished, no one really cares because it was so long ago since you set off!

Once the idea was conceived and the plan had started to take some sort of shape, it was now down to me. I needed to get my body from a 14.5 stone back row forward to the body of an endurance athlete in about 6 months. "It's all about the core," she screeched as I punished myself on the treadmill for another 3 hours – the unmistakable voice of Jane Peggs barking across the gym. Like me, Jane also takes great pride in keeping herself in shape, even more so for Jane as this has not always been the case. I think Jane is probably one of the fittest 70 year olds (sorry Jane) on the face of the planet. Her strength, determination and drive are amazing; she is an inspiration to many. I think this is the reason we have such a terrific friendship.

My training went from a weight session a few times a week and a bit of touch rugby, to something that most would deem torture. I was lifting heavy weights 4 times a week, trying hard to keep some muscle mass, as I knew my body would start to eat at this. I was taking 7 kettle-bell sessions a week with a massive amount of core exercises thrown in here, as well. If people have ever wondered how I managed to keep going, just grab a kettle-bell and get swinging! It's a brutal mix of cardio and weight training. I was also running further and further. I was running small 10 milers, every other day during the week, then on a weekend taking it right up to 30 miles or over. Even then, I still needed to be stronger, to be fitter. Keeping good weight and shedding the bad has never been too much of a problem for me. I have always wanted to be heavier for the rugby team, but it never really happened like that. I suppose when I look at it now, my body was built for endurance!

I have read a lot of other books about running and how people manage to keep their minds busy while they are running, or doing whatever they are doing. I have watched as many tried and failed. I knew I had one thing that would keep driving me forward – my fear of failing; the feeling of letting so many people down. Before, when I have quit or given up on something, it has not been something that affected that many people; this time it actually meant something. I have read a lot about success and I have watched videos about motivation.

Many of you may be reading this, saying, "I don't have time to work out." You are lying to yourself. I hate to tell, you but if you want to make it, it's bloody hard graft! Ask yourself this: would you choose sleep over success? Did you need 30 minutes extra sleep, or could you have spent that time running, cycling or doing something towards making yourself successful and achieving your goals?!

CHAPTER 4

Choosing Help for Heroes

It wasn't a particularly difficult choice for me to choose *Help for Heroes* to support. Having served myself, it is something I have always wanted to try and help with. The war in Afghanistan has certainly brought the horrific injuries sustained by some of our servicemen and women into the mainstream media. As a rugby man, many of my friends and team mates have served in many locations all over the world and I am sure we are all aware of someone in our community who has been affected by war.

It was seeing documentaries on the TV that inspired me even more. I have both my arms and legs, as I am sure many people reading this do, and yet I can easily spend the majority of my time sat down moaning about something that really doesn't matter. I was asked why I run. Simple! I run for those who can't.

So everyone knew who I was running for. I had my van plastered with every single sign, flag or banner that I could possibly fit onto the side of it. The van would sleep two people, albeit two very small people! It was a

"J" registered VW van that was about to drive 2,500 miles, going less than 10 miles an hour the entire way. My hopes for the van making it back without breaking down were low. Banners saying what I was doing adorned the van: 'Beep for Support' and 'Sam Boatwright, 50 miles for 50 days'. Whether you agree with the war or not, whether you believe the Government should be doing more to help our injured personnel, it didn't matter; right now they need our help and I was going to do whatever it took to help them.

CHAPTER 5

The Kit

From the point of view of those ultra athletes that might be reading this I imagine this section will be of relative interest. For those that have no idea about running (me not too long ago) then trainers and running tights are the same no matter what. For the non runners, you might choose your attire in a number of different ways, colour, brand, size, warmth, cost or all of the above. Whichever way you decide it's probably not because you are about to run 2500 miles in it. I had to be very "kit" smart. Unfortunately I still had constraints, such as cost and weight. I couldn't just shoot to the shops and buy the most expensive kit on the market as I was struggling to pay bill and other expenses for the run already. Whatever I chose needed to be durable but also not chafe! Chaffage is a runner's nightmare and once it's in grained its unbelievably painful for a long time. Anything from your underwear to the hat on your head can cause it.

I had plenty of time to test my kit, I had done hundreds of practice runs and worn many different clothes but I still had my favourites. I had asked my running coach

Chris to watch me run over a longer distance to ensure my choice of trainer was correct. The Mizuno Nirvana 7 was the choice, it had great balance, light but sturdy with great cushion for pounding the tarmac. Even now I still wear them, they are a superb trainer and not one that would have been my first choice but with a little conversation from the salesman in the running shop it was the Nirvana 7's that got my vote. A slight geekness shone through with this purchase, not only were they the best trainer for me but also Nirvana are and always will be my favourite band. Many would just call it noise, me, it's the sound of my youth. The screaming angered and gravelled voice of Kurt Cobain, pulses as I run.

For the non runner and the runners among you, "Joggers Nipple" is almost a common phrase. If this is a phrase that is alien to you, you are very lucky. Joggers Nipple is like rubbing your nipples with sand paper and every now and again letting a small trickle of salty sweat run over the red roar body parts. I can see many of you wincing at the thought of it. Trust me, it is not pleasant. I had to wear clothing that would minimize the risk. A lot of runners out there use plasters over their nipples to ensure this doesn't happen but due to the amount of sweat that protrudes from me with any exercise I thought it best to wear a top that glided over the top rather than eroded them off. I wore what's called an under armour skin or "warm top". These tops are designed to either keep you warm or keep you cool. I always wear the warm top even when it's warm. It keeps my core muscles warm all the time. Whether its scientific fact or not I feel better knowing that my core is warm, it helped my back muscles stay loose when pounding the road and enabled me to wear whatever I felt like over the top. On particularly warm days I would wear the under armour top alone, but on colder days I would layer up over the top of it. Vests, hoodies, t shirts or even another under armour top with longer sleeves would be worn just to try and stay warm. Most of the run was cold and wet and the good thing about under armour clothing is that it dries very fast. During breaks in my running if the weather was nice the van would look like a mobile clothes horse as my kit adorned the windows as I tried to dry it out.

My bottom half was the same every day. Only once on the entire run did I try and wear shorts and it proved to be a nightmare. I wore Nike Dri Fit tights as these like the under armour were great for keeping my muscles warm. It's always been my theory that if I can keep my muscles warm even at a slower pace I was less likely to pull something. As the pace was slow my body would never get so warm that I was over heating so I no problems with this. I needed something that would stop my legs chafing against each other and also remain light enough when they were wet. The Nike tights were amazing they did exactly what they said.

My underwear and socks were of vital importance, as many have found blisters are a constant battle but not something I have ever suffered with too much. 1000 Mile socks were the answer to everything for me. Two thin layers of fabric resulting in no blisters at all, not one. I would occasionally switch to Nike Dri fit socks if the rain was so intense that I feared my clothing would become saturated. The Dri Fits worked as they kept my feet dry. I am sure there are many people out there already cursing me as they have tried the same and then still got blisters, for this all I can say is that it worked for me. The advice I would give people is to try a few out and hopefully through trial and error you will find the best for you. Unfortunately this can be a very painful process.

Throughout the run I was very careful about my boxer shorts. Even something simple, not quite getting a seam in the right or slightly twisted in places can have catastrophic circumstances. The chafing in this area (details not needed) can be severe and sometimes end a run. Sara (my wife) worked for Fat Face, a well respected high street chain who sells top quality clothing. Fat Face management had already sponsored me and also allowed Sara to take a longer than normal holiday to help support me. The discount Sara got from the store allowed me to purchase a large amount of boxer shorts at a great price. I did every single training run in these and I ran everyday of the 50 days in a pair of Fat Face boxer shorts. Not once did they let me down. Epic boxer shorts.

CHAPTER 6

Excitement, Enthusiasm
and Trepidation

April 6, 2012. Blackpool: 8am.

Friday, 6th April 2012 – Mum, Dad, Trev, Harriet, Sara, Auntie Glen, Uncle Ian, Emily, Andy (my driver) and I, stood outside the Sandcastle Swimming Pool in Blackpool and it was bloody freezing! Picture this: the wind is blowing straight down the promenade at me and I am already thinking, "Bloody Hell, 50 miles is a really long way!" Pushing out of Blackpool, I run along the sea front by myself, it's great, lots of other runners and cyclists. It's great to feel part of a small community of people. Many of you might call them nutters! People you see out in all weathers, trudging through the rain or snow for no other reason other than to get some fresh air and keep fit.

Chest out and I am almost strutting down the promenade. I feel great. I have Kasabian's *Underdog* hammering through my earphones which, like the title suggests, I feel like. I am the underdog. Nobody expects me to complete this challenge. I am running 8 minute miles and pushing hard through my toes, heading north towards today's final goal of Carnforth. Nothing much is passing through my mind. I am taking in the sights and sounds of Blackpool, loving being on the road and to have finally set my feet going on my massive challenge. I feel on top of the world! I am leaving behind me everything that is normal and heading towards something completely unknown – towards undoubted pain and mental torture! At this moment in time, none of that is even near to my mind. All I can do is smile and push hard.

It is strange how much one random act of kindness can change a day, whether it is a donation from a stranger, to the beep of a car horn. It is these random acts of kindness that make the world a better place. If every person strived to do this once a day, we might possibly live in a much friendlier and more sociable universe. Having so many people toot their horns, donate money, clap, shout, cheer and wave made every stride feel good. Made every stride feel like I was making a difference and that I knew people were right behind what I was doing.

There were quite a few things that I needed to sort out. Mainly when I should stop for food and when I could pull over to grab a drink. The roads on a Bank Holiday are torture. It was near impossible to stop anywhere with many of the roads around Blackpool and Fleetwood, crammed full with traffic. I did manage to do a radio interview while running which also helped me get some more toots and waves from passing traffic.

I knew I wasn't eating correctly, but I felt great; I was running hard and going really well. I was well up on my pace and nothing was hurting. The miles shot by with the passing landscape. I thought of all the people stuck in their cars looking at me thinking, "There goes another runner, but why is he running up this busy road when there are beautiful paths all over?" I wanted to shout to everyone just how far I was going and exactly what I had started. Support on the run was something I was going to need a massive amount of, whether it was from friends or family. I didn't want to admit it to anyone, but I was scared. I could not fail this time.

CHAPTER 7

The best laid plans and all that rubbish!

So what exactly is pain? The people of Grange-Over-Sands probably think that pain equates to a lot of swear words! I could not think of any way of getting through the day without swearing. Every footstep was welcomed with excruciating pain straight through my heel and into my knees. My stomach burned with pain like pokers were stuck between every rib, all because I was stupid and thought I could run without refueling. I remember cursing myself on every stride, "Stupid, stupid, stupid idiot!" These words repeated on my mind all the way through the day. Reflecting on that second day, I now know it was one of the toughest throughout the entire run! Andy tried his hardest to keep me going; he did everything he could. In the end, I asked him to leave me to go on by myself for a few miles, unsupported. I wanted to curl up in a little ball and cry. Tears rolled down my face as I imagined all the people I would let down when I failed. All the people back at home that had backed me and believed in me. I have broken bones playing rugby, I have had operations to my ankles and my shoulder from injuries - this pain was worse! From my toes to the hair on my head, everything hurt. Downhill was worse than anything, and for those of you aware of the Cumbrian landscape, down-hills are a fairly regular occurrence. When travelling down-hill, there is three times your own body weight going through your knee and ankle joints. The constant pounding from the previous day had enflamed my ligaments and my knees and ankles had swollen. Anti-Inflammatory tablets were consumed at a rate that would not sit well with most medical advisors, but I needed them. Whether it was more a state of mind or not, I found that they were helping.

The landscape of Cumbria is truly spectacular! It's not the same as the Yorkshire Dales. It has its own unique aura that completely engrosses you until you find yourself almost in a daydream while you tootle along. This was just what I needed; something to take my mind away. Rolling hills undulated all the way to the coast line and it was almost a pleasure to feel part of that landscape.

Andy tried to regiment my eating. He would drive on ahead of me for a few miles and boil up a massive vat of pasta, like we were feeding the 5,000. It's how imagine prison food (no offence Andy). The campervan had the most basic amenities: gas stove, sink, cupboards and a toilet. It worked well. Andy was fantastic for keeping me going and ensuring that I ate well and got plenty of fluid on. He would tell me stories of his life and the things he had done. I loved it! This was what I needed, having someone talk to me so I didn't have to think; I could just listen. The weather was pretty kind for the most part – a few rain and hail showers, but nothing too dramatic.

I was still unsure how to break each day up; I was just running until I was hungry or getting tired, then stopped for something to eat. It's a strange feeling having no barrier no real goal. At the start of the day, your goal is to complete 50 miles, but you know that you can't just blast out the entire 50, so you try and break it down. A little bit of trial and error was needed. The only problem being was when we made an 'error', they were costly. It could be something stupid like running a bit too fast, or maybe even not eating at the right time. Whichever one it was, my body was very quick to let me know I had made a mistake.

Arriving in Barrow, you get a feeling of how much the place depended on ship building. Much of the town is in ruin apart from a brand new retail park which looks amazingly out of place within its vernacular. Barrow is fighting to stay alive; it is trying hard to keep up, but I got the feeling that the fight was almost over. The people, buildings, even the pigeons look beaten and tired. Life is hard in Barrow.

As we had the campervan, the plan was to run the 50 miles every day and then, wherever we were, stop and sleep for the night. This was something that in planning sounded awesome – almost romanticizing the challenge a little. What more could you want than to pull over in a little country lay by and cook a lovely meal on a little hob? Peace and quiet! But that didn't happen – ever ! Sweat and tears had poured out of me during the day and all I wanted was to get clean: a shower, bath – even a large sink would do. We stopped at a guest house in Barrow. I use the term 'guest house' very loosely. This was not a place you would have visited with a loved one, or even someone you hated for that matter. The receptionist/bouncer was easily over 6'6", with a shaven head uncovering a wealth of scars; his hands looked like shovels intertwined with tattoos of daggers and naked ladies. As I went to sign in, the gargantuan handed me a pen which looked more like a cocktail stick in the hands of a gorilla. I nervously took the pen and was half tempted to write a fake name! I certainly never wanted this guy following me.

The website of the guest house suggested that there had been recent renovations! I can only imagine what the place must have been like before. Wall paper hung off the walls, the little bit that still clung to the wall covered yellow stained damp plaster. From my point of view, it was a bed –admittedly, probably a bed where a murder had taken place, but still a bed. I laid on the bed and sank about a foot; I was probably 2 inches off the floor! I smiled – 'the rock and roll lifestyle', I thought to myself, as I jiggled and gyrated myself back off the bed. I stepped cautiously into the shower which seemed basic – 'On ' and 'Off'. The water came out at a rate that I could produce when spitting; the only problem was that these drops were like being spat at with volcanic lava. Off, off, off, off. I pressed the button about 100 times with my body pushed against the back of the shower cubicle to try and avoid the boiling water drops. Eventually it turned off, my body screaming in pain from the run, now had a little bit extra to contend with. The sink was used instead! A fly on the wall in that bathroom would have died laughing as my 6'3" frame maneuvered myself to wash all important bits in a sink that was the size of two large apples.

Bed at last.

CHAPTER 8

What a difference a day makes!

I have heard the expression 'what a difference a day makes' never really thinking much about it. When you are running day after day, it is one that sticks in your mind constantly. Each day brings with it something new, some new challenge, be it a new pain somewhere in the body, or some mental hurdle that you have to overcome. It was Easter Sunday. I had set off with a number of packages that I was not allowed to open until Easter day, so I had guessed that they were likely to be chocolate. Thankfully, I was not wrong! As I scoffed my way through another bar of chocolate, I started to think about everyone sat at home eating their Easter Eggs. It was weird how much I missed home; just having people around you who love and support you, no matter what, makes a big difference. I had only been running 3 days and I was already missing home a lot.

I cracked on through the morning at a really good pace, attacking each climb with a renewed vengeance. I hit a large climb and as it peaked, I could see right across the valley. It was a spectacular view to behold! Way down in the bottom of the valley, I saw a red van. The only reason it stuck out so much was that I hadn't seen many cars that morning and I thought to myself, "My Dad has a van like that." As I ascended the hill, I realised that it was my Mum and Dad. It made my day! Mum even donned her running gear and stuck with me for a few miles while my dad followed closely on his bike. My Dad stuck with us for a while before heading back to the van to catch us up again.

Running alone is a very lonely thing to do, so having my parents there –even for a few hours – was fantastic. It meant that three hours sailed by. While they were with me, we hit some really heavy climbs. Mum decided that climbing was not for her and fell back to the support vehicle (campervan) and waited till more 'Mum friendly' running was available.

It was on the 3rd day that I made one very important observation which informed the rest of the run. Where ever you see a sign for a castle, there is going to be an almighty hill! The reason that castle is still there is because the enemy were probably too tired to climb up the damn hill it was built on! This not so startling discovery was made in Cumbria, which in comparison to Scotland, had relatively few castles. I didn't know much about Scotland; the furthest north I had been was Edinburgh, but one thing I did know was – there were a lot of Castles! It was going to hurt – a lot!

Running was good all day. Andy even spurred me up a couple of steeper climbs, peeping the horn and turning Status Quo up to deafening volumes in the campervan behind me, *Rocking All Over the World* blaring out across the Cumbrian countryside – and I was loving it. Due to the sheer volume of climbs, my feet were taking a battering. I hadn't really thought too much about my feet up until that point, but I could start to feel a squelching feeling in my trainer as if I stood in a puddle. I continued running, just putting it down to sweat. It wasn't until I took my trainer off later that night that I noticed I had lost three toe nails – one on my left foot and two on my right. Removing my sock was horrible! Layers of skin left with the sock and a wave of pain hit my body when I saw my foot.

One thing I had kept in my mind the whole of the day was knowing that, no matter what, I was having a bath when I got in. No checking into hotels or washing my boxer shorts in the sink, as I was staying with a friend of a friend in Whitehaven. It was a gorgeous little town that couldn't come soon enough. The rain had started to land quite heavy in the late afternoon. I had been on the road for 10 hours, but made great progress. Julie came to meet me on the road and we followed her back to her house. Once the iodine had been sprayed on my foot and the pain killers choked down, I laid in the bath, wincing every time I moved my feet. Rather melodramatically, I thought about soldiers on the front line in World War II who had suffered with trench foot and all manner of horrible ailments and diseases. It was also about this time I gave myself a right good kick up the arse and told myself to man up! I suppose you can't really feel sorry for yourself laid in a bath full of bubbles!

Julie had made enough spaghetti bolognese to ensure Italy would never go hungry again; my plate was heaped full, and I half contemplated asking for a doggy bag. I think Julie thought that I had lost a lot of weight while I was running. I did try and explain that this was only the third day and that I may lose some weight, but at the moment I was going pretty well. Apple pie and custard followed. My stomach felt like I had ingested a beach ball as I made my way to bed. I collapsed into the bed and had a great night's sleep – a perfect end to a great day's running.

CHAPTER 9

They sound Scottish?

Heading out on day 4, I felt a new confidence building in me. The last 2 days had been hard going and although I knew there would be much harder things to come, I felt proud that I had dealt with some quite severe pain and battled through it.

I was getting regular updates from home; my brother (Trev) called most days to check my progress and I usually spoke to him a few times in a day, especially on a weekend. It was great to speak to people on the phone as I knew I was running round about 10 minute miles, so if I could keep someone on the phone for longer than 20 minutes, I would have done at least 2 miles. Every little goal made the miles pass that little bit easier. My running coach, Chris Carniss (a former professional marathon runner) gave me tips on how to pass time. Counting my strides was a big one for me. I would count every left foot stride knowing that 600 of them would be about a 1 mile run. What usually happened was that I would get to about 3 or 4 hundred and then someone would call, or I would lose concentration and forget where I had got up to. I still always knew I was about half way which meant I had done at least half a mile.

I was heading up towards Scotland on England's west coast. Tonight I would be stopping in one of the last towns before Scotland. I knew I would be traversing Scotland for about the next two and a half weeks which was slightly daunting, but also something I was relishing at the same time. Scotland is a place completely alien to me. I have never really been too far north, but I have just been told of its amazing, natural beauty. So far, there was no argument that anywhere I had been did not have something truly beautiful about it. Even Blackpool, all those 200 miles back down the coast, has something quite romantic and beautiful about it.

Longtown is a place unlike any other and I know this can be said for a lot of places, but I think Longtown could even be its own country! The language and dialect of the people there is part Scottish, part Cumbrian and part Clingon I think. Never in my life have I said pardon so many times. I remember when I first went to visit my younger brother in Newcastle while he was at university there. We went for dinner in a small bakery and I went to pay for our meal. The waitress said something to me and, to this day, I don't have a clue what she said. I stood with a glazed look on my face and made the social faux pas of asking her to repeat herself about 7 times. Eventually my brother screamed at me, "Just give her the money mate!" Apparently, she was saying £7.79! This same uncomfortable social situation arose in Longtown. Walking into a pub which we believed would sell food – and why wouldn't it – said, 'Food Served all day'! Just as everyone in the pub stopped talking, we walked nervously to the bar. My voice broke as I asked for a menu. "We don't do food," barked the 'thing' from behind the bar. Our exit was rapid! Luckily, another hostelry was serving and we duly plunged our way through three courses.

When doing anything, I always like to set goals for myself; they can be goals for a day, week, month or even a year. Whatever your goals are, stick to them. One of my first major goals, aside from not dropping to my knees and crying like a baby, was to make it all the way to Scotland and I had done it! As the signs for Gretna counted down the mileage, I remember thinking how amazing it was to be crossing into another country and I wondered how foreign people felt when they were visiting the UK. I have to be honest, it was a bit of an anti-climax! I don't really know what I had expected – maybe for my body to have a breath of new energy, or maybe some mystical Scottish magic to make me feel revived and revitalized. Sadly, this was not the case. In fact, the rest of the day was a bit of a battle against the elements. It chucked everything at us! I went from short sleeves to full rain gear in a matter of miles.

Out of the days run so far, I knew that today I had to hit my target. The other days were important as I needed to keep on track, but today more so, due to the fact that my drivers were swapping over and I was getting a new driver. Andy had been brilliant. It's always tough spending 24 hours a day in isolation. Even though I was isolated, out running all day – in all weathers – I forgot that my drivers were isolated too. They had minimal human contact all day. It was great at the end of the day to have a sit down with Andy and just find out about his life, the things he had done and the places he had been. I enjoyed just sitting, listening to his stories and not having to come up with replies. Andy figured out very quickly that I can sit and listen to him for hours, but I was physically and emotionally shattered, so he never expected a real, life-changing conversation!

The run was sapping everything I had. My own mental strength was drained daily and every night it needed to be replenished. At the end of day 5, Tom arrived. Like Andy, Tom was a guy I knew, but not someone I knew too well. It's how I wanted things really; if I had brought only people I knew, they would soon run out of conversation. Andy gave Tom a run-down of the types of things we had been doing and what I had been eating. I was sad to see Andy go, but I also knew that, like me, he was shattered as well.

CHAPTER 10

Pain is temporary?
Have you tried running?

Most people that have ever run any distance have heard of Dean Karnezes. I read Dean's books before I set off, to try and gain a little inspiration and also a little bit of knowledge of how to deal with things. The truth is, there is no way for someone to tell you how to deal with pain. You will hear it all…

- Pain is temporary
- Pain is your friend
- Harness the pain
- Pain is weakness leaving the body

The brutal facts are – pain hurts! It's how you deal with pain that makes you what you are. I am described as being a runner with a rugby player's attitude. This attitude tends to push your body through anything to keep it going. Your body is simply a tool, or you are just a piece of meat. I believe that all rugby players have that stubbornness, a sheer bloody-mindedness to never show weakness.

Scotland will find your weaknesses! Making my way up the Solway Coast, pain ate at me all day. It not only takes its toll on your body, but your mind grows weary of having to deal with pain. Blocking things out is an art form; it is something I can do easily. My body can do one thing while my mind is somewhere else. Any challenge needs this sort of mind set. The mindset that says whatever happens, you have to keep going.

It was day 6 where doubt really did set in. Shooting pains through my knees from enflamed ligaments around the joint hurt badly. It was awful. Pain so bad, that, with each step, everything hurt! Screams of agony were being belted out regularly, each scream representing enough pain to draw tears. Tears were shed on a regular basis; if you think yourself too manly to cry, try doing anything that pushes you to your limits and you will soon see that tears are just a way of getting through.

Tom did everything he could to keep me going in Scotland and bar getting out of the van and physically carrying me, there was not much else he could do. As I have already mentioned, it was great to see the generosity of the public. This was never more present than when I was hobbling into Wigtown at the end of the day. I had about 6 miles left to run. It was about 6.15 in the evening and I had been on the road since 7am. The day had been a blur of painkillers, big hills, searing pain and breathtaking views. There is a small winding road leading into Wigtown and the pain was becoming quite severe. I had just hobbled across a busy part of the road when I got a text on my phone asking if I was in Wigtown. I was, I replied. It was from someone I worked with that wouldn't usually text me, so I thought it was quite strange. The reply came back:

"Just passed you on the way into Wigtown. You looked in agony. KEEP GOING BIG MAN!"

That text was enough for me to get me through those last few miles. It turned out my friends were visiting family in the area. Small world.

After the torture of the previous days, I needed to get some much needed medical advice. I rang my very wise friend Jane Peggs, the' Fairy Godmother' of running. She suggested that I no longer take the pain killers and anti-inflammatories as a cure for the pain, but instead use it as a course of medication to prevent it happening again, or in simply summary – PREVENTION RATHER THAN CURE. Damn...she is good!! Although, the pain persisted, it became more something I had to deal with, rather than something that was stopping me from moving.

Waking up in Wigtown was pretty strange; there is not a whole lot of stuff to do there to be honest! It is very famous for bookshops and there were plenty of them. The hotel was good and they were able to supply ice. Although I think the bar man thought I was a little crazy when I asked for 10 pints of ice!

Setting off, Tom and I decided that we needed a touch more exposure and we also wanted to give the growing social media network something to look at, so we decided to make a video. The first video on tour was the 'Plank-Press Up'. A brutal combination leading from plank then walking your hands up into a press up position, completing a full press up (chest to the floor) and then back on to your elbows! It hurts! Without doubt it is tough, and coupled with a cold Scottish April morning and a rather unforgiving pavement, it made for great watching!

We pushed hard out of Wigtown, a small breeze at my back and we carried on right up to mid-morning. I broke the day down into manageable chunks. Today was two sections of 13.5 miles and then the afternoon would be broken down into 3 or 4 stops, depending on how I was feeling.

CHAPTER *11*

A change is as good as a break

One thing I learnt quite fast when running all day is that sleep is well up there with nutrition as one of the most important things. We stayed in a small hotel right next to the main road. It looked peaceful enough and it was, until a coach party arrived that were heading down to Aintree to go to the races!! Where they had come from God only knows?! However, this was their halfway point and so they stopped at the same hotel as us. At one point during the night, I could have sworn that 2 of the 'ladies' were about to come crashing through the wall.

As we settled down for breakfast the next morning, all the coach party were there, pint of lager in hand ready for the next stint of their journey. I imagine they didn't even notice the amazingly pasty, white guy with the massive ginger beard and running tights sat right next to them. Tom arrived for breakfast a couple of minutes later; he too looked equally as rough with the lack of sleep, but he was happy as we had hit 400 likes on *Facebook* which was what he had been hoping to achieve. I liked the fact that Tom had become involved in the run, as at the last minute, he made a huge difference and made me smile everyday with his commentary on the camera and his positive attitude.

Tom, like me, had fallen in love with Scotland. It was somewhere he had spent a lot of time. Quite often when stopping for a break, we would try and get to a clearing, where there would be hardly any words spoken, but we could just sit and stare and take it all in. I usually sat and thought about the millions of people all over who were not able to be looking at what I was looking at.

When I lost my first toenails it was quite painful ; by now I had none. The painful part was putting a sock on in the morning and taking it off again at night. It's quite hard to describe the feeling, but it feels like constantly stubbing your toe. I am sure we have all done it; you stub your toe on the castor, of the sofa, or on the coffee table or something your kids have left out. Immediately a swear word enters your head and this is usually followed by an expletive at the inanimate object you just whacked your toe on! Well, imagine stubbing your toe at least twice a day!

CHAPTER *12*

Painkillers,
protein shakes and PMA

Scotland is an amazing country with lots of things to see and do; it has great history and traditions and it really is somewhere everyone should visit. I would, however, not visit Irvine. Apologies to the people of Irvine, as you guys were spectacular, but the city just seemed so lonely and run down. It needs a social defibrillator! I left Irvine as quickly as I had arrived, with Kate now driving as we headed up through Glasgow, across the Erskine Bridge and into Dumbarton.

I can safely say that as a very proud Englishman and Yorkshire man, I was crapping myself going through Glasgow. Today, as I sit and write, I have no idea why, but I guess like anywhere, Glasgow has a reputation and it's not one of peace and tranquility or free love for all. Its reputation is like its building – hard concrete. Running through the centre of the city, you are fully aware of how hard life is, and what it takes to survive. Boarded up windows and shattered glass are common place, but within this hard exterior are a few diamonds in the rough. The Erskine Bridge, in my opinion, is one of them. It towers into the sky with its massive structure and, as a man who prefers to keep his feet on solid ground, it felt amazing to go across it and just look back over the city.

There have been many times while on my run that I have been referred to as 'Forrest Gump'. This may be quite fitting, but I am fairly positive that Forrest's idea of 'just running' had a few monumental flaws! One of which is where the hell you go to the toilet? When in the country side, it's easy, or as easy as it can be outside, squatting away from public view. However, whilst you are in the public view, it's a lot more difficult. This was never more apparent than when I ran through Dumbarton. Dumbarton was my final stop that day. It had been a tough day and the pain killers were playing havoc with my stomach. I decided I couldn't keep going for the last few miles and that I needed to use the dreaded chemical toilet. I am 6' 3" inches tall, and the toilet is less than 1 foot tall. Getting on to the toilet is a challenge in itself, but getting off the damn thing is something else entirely. Dumbarton was different though. Pulling in to Dumbarton, the need for a toilet grew, but I had only just come off of the Erksine Bridge and knew we were still in a built up area, so the chemical toilet it would have to be. We pulled in. I managed to get on the toilet and sat, as you do, contemplating life, God and the universe, while nature took its course. As things were coming to an end, I heard some voices. I looked out of the window and realised there were quite a few people amassing. I looked out of another window straight into the face of an elderly lady!!

She smiled, then, as she looked further down my body very slowly, the smile suddenly disappeared! I quickly realised we had pulled into a bus stop!! "KATE!!!" I yelled! My driver, Kate, had made herself scarce due to the reason for stopping. We belted off down the street, my pace much quicker than at any other time on the run.

It's always hard waking up when you know a day is going to be hard. In the planning stages of the run, I looked at the elevations and this was one of the toughest climbs going. A climb called *Rest and be Thankful*. It was aptly named due to the length of the climb (about 7miles) and also its gradient – about a constant 12%. Like anything in life, if you know something horrible is coming up, your natural instinct is to try and get away from it; unfortunately for me, this couldn't happen!! Straight up was the only way up, and what a horrible way it was! Sara (my wife) ran with me this morning which was ace; it really does make a difference having someone with you that will just try and keep you going. Sara had her own goals which was to try and run her first marathon, but unfortunately, due to my pace and pain, it was only about 23 miles.

Heading out of Dumbarton was great; a local lady came to run with us whose name I still to this day cannot work out. She asked what we were doing and whether I was mad; as usual, I replied, "No, I'm not mad – just thought I would go for a little jog." Running with us for about 5 miles, the lady told me and Sara all about why she ran and what it meant to her. I love hearing why people run. Sometimes it's not just about fitness, but getting a part of yourself back. No phones, meetings, relationships – just you and the pavement.

Sara left at dinner time and was replaced by my eldest brother, Trev. His real name is Matthew, but everyone calls him Trev. I had to add this section as my Mum wanted to make sure that everyone knows that she has not named her son Trevor. Apologies if you are called Trevor! As with Sara's arrival, Trev's had the same effect on me. It gave me a massive boost to want to keep going and push on towards the top of Scotland.

Inveraray was a cold and damp place to start out from. Well into my second week of running, the nerves were starting to grow and common sense told me that the pain might become too much to bear. I was not getting out of bed like I normally would now; it had turned into a full scale military operation. Keeping my legs as straight as I could, I would roll to the side and slowly bend onto my knees. There was a large debate when writing this book whether swear words should be added, as it was my argument that in order to fully understand the pain I was in, then swear words were needed… so feel free to add lots of swear words right now ………………….

Heading out of Inveraray, I realized how isolated the village/town was. It sat right on the side of the loch in the most picturesque location, the type you would send on a postcard of Scotland. I had not really appreciated its beauty on the way in the night before, due to my legs and feet feeling like they were about to explode. I headed north out of Inveraray, pushing up towards Inverness and Loch Ness. My target for the day was really to keep going on the first section for as long as my legs would allow and then hit the afternoon with some force to try and clock the miles. Once again, the plans for the day were changed quite massively after the first 3 miles.

Climbing out of Inveraray was horrible – quiet, Scottish roads that dragged on for miles with no areas to sit and enjoy a view. The trees that lined the roads were thick and miles deep; indeed, an almost creepy eeriness befell the road. I felt like I was running in an American horror movie! This feeling was not helped by my brother, who amused himself by hanging out of the window of the campervan and howling like a werewolf. I would then get a text on my phone...

"MESSAGE FROM TREV: "I think I just saw a werewolf!"

I would read the message, and look back at the van to see my brother in tears of laughter. People ask whether I went crazy on the run and whether my mind played tricks on me. I didn't need my mind to play tricks on me when I had him behind me!

Once the climbing was done, the roads seemed to drag on for miles with no semblance of life apart from the odd sheep or cow. Step after step and mile after mile I trudged on through the harsh Scottish landscape. The monotony of the road was only broken by the odd drinks break and a quick pee at the side of the road. Pee stops were quite normal at the side of the road, but Trev decided that they were not quite amusing enough, so while I peed, he would sit in the van and toot the horn the entire time, just in case there was anyone passing!

I had downloaded a *'Learn to Speak Spanish'* application on my phone as I thought it would be very amusing for me to learn some and then jump back in the van when I was on a break and speak Spanish. The idea and the result were very different; there is not much point in jumping back into the campervan and asking where the train station is, or how to order two beers. However, Spanish lessons continued most of the day.

As we headed further north, the thick forests that lined the road thinned and cleared away to reveal amazing panoramic views that had every type of landscape – from vast lochs to sweeping hills – all shadowed by snowcapped mountains in the distance. It was these snowcapped mountains that I was heading towards. At times, I was down to little more than a walk; the earlier climbs had beaten my legs until they had little left in them. A phrase often used is 'a second wind'. Well, I was on the 'one hundredth wind', and the pain was still a constant.

CHAPTER 13

Surely, it's false advertising?

Fort William is a gorgeous little town sat at the foot of Ben Nevis surrounded by smaller hills and mountains and with the loch running right alongside. It really is breath taking! I am sure throughout my time in Scotland, I will run out of ways to describe its beauty.

Fort William is the town marketed as 'Ben Nevis Town', which is kind of funny, as you can't actually see Ben Nevis from Fort William!! We certainly couldn't anyway, due to the amount of rain and snow that was pelting our window when we woke up. Today was Trev's last day. We had stopped in a hotel next to a whiskey distillery, the smell of which is one that once in your nasal passage, takes some shifting.

I had visited a physio on my arrival into Fort William the previous evening. My knees and ankles were swelling to a point that anti-inflammatory pain killers were redundant. The reaction of Jacqui Parfitt (physio in Fort William) assured me that I was not being soft and that it was probably a good idea to be there.

"That is certainly not supposed to look like that," said Jacqui, an English woman who had moved to Scotland with her husband.

"No, it does hurt a bit when I press through it on a climb, but that's nothing compared to my ankle," I said, showing the swollen lump on the aforementioned.

The conversation continued like this as I listed my various ailments. As Jacqui carefully, albeit brutally, massaged my aching muscles, the doubt that had begun the previous day began to creep back in as to whether the pain really would become too much. Could I really block it out and press on? With so many people who believed in me who could to be proved so wrong.

I pressed hard out of Fort William, into driving snow which was horrifically cold on my face and hands. I covered as much of my skin as I could until just my eyes peaked through. Pace was good due to the temperature; I knew I had to keep pushing hard to keep my body warm. Visibility was near zero, so Trev went ahead in the campervan to make a brew a few miles down the road. This was always the hardest part. Alone on the road with no one, and people looking at me like I had escaped from somewhere, always thinking, "Why would you run in this?" As I climbed out of Fort William, I saw a monument at the top which is dedicated to fallen marines. It had a wreath of poppies round it. I stopped and swept the snow to the side and read some of the names. Seeing this was just what I needed – something to give me a kick to let me know that although it was cold and my legs were hurting, somewhere, someone was hurting worse than me.

I wouldn't exactly say I sprinted away, but there was certainly more of a spring in my step. I saw the weather was just something else to challenge me and I also knew that the people who were passing me could see my dedication to this challenge. At the brew stop, I needed to get changed as my clothes were saturated, and on my rapidly decreasing frame, it felt like I was dragging another person along with me.

I was so excited to see Loch Ness. It may sound quite childish, but I still believe every person that passes it believes that it's their day and that they will see Nessie! I was definitely going to have ample time next to the loch in any case, as I would running the length of the Loch for the remainder of the day and then just a little bit more up to Inverness for the night. It was fantastic to be running this road and have the loch by my side for the entire day, but it was also dangerous. Logging wagons fly along the road and I don't think a small Yorkshireman in tights is what they normally expect to see. A couple of times, evasive action was very necessary; this included a rather soggy ditch jump followed by standing in one of the largest puddles ever seen on a road! The very same puddle was then blasted all up my front as the wagon I was evading drove through the puddle. Change of clothes number 2 followed!

Arriving in Inverness was great. My Mum and Dad had spent the day driving up to meet us and I had been constantly on the phone. What had taken me almost 2 weeks to run, my dad had driven in about 9 hours! Unfortunately for him, he was now about to turn round to take Trev back home and drop off my Mum, who

I hadn't seen since Cumbria. I was tired and I was hurting and my Mum knew that I was close to breaking point.

The hotel in Inverness was amazing; they cleaned and dried my sodden clothes and the meal was exactly what I needed.

Sleep, too, was also needed.

I had been tinkering around with different ways of running, which to the hardened professional will probably sound stupid, but I wanted to try run the bulk of the miles before lunch, and then gently wind down through the afternoon. I was always better first thing - painkillers had settled into my body and the previous night's ice bath had soothed what they could of my aching muscles; moreover, every day I woke up, I was somewhere I had never been before.

The target for the day was Elgin. This would mean passing RAF Lossiemouth which was the most northern point on the run and so a small milestone to achieve. Hammering out 35 miles at a faster pace meant that the afternoon and evening sessions were quite pleasant in comparison. This would definitely be the way forward for me. It meant that by the time I came to finish in an evening, I would be at a very slow jog and already on the wind down.

The day was gorgeous; the sun shone throughout the entire day and made the running all the more pleasant. Many people have said to me that they prefer to run in the rain. I always smile and say, "Yes, it is nice," but once you have done it for 3 days continuously, it becomes a tad irritating to say the least.

Once again, my Fairy God Mother, Jane Peggs, sent me some strapping tape with my Mum. The 'care packages' from home made a huge difference. The strapping tape is brilliant, as it allows decent movement and doesn't itch; the only problem is that it's expensive! As half of my body was covered in blue tape, I probably looked to most people like some kind of reject Egyptian Mummy! The difference was incredible, though. My knees felt better as there was no lateral movement now and the swelling on my ankle was controllable with the tape. The doubts that were in my mind were slowly dissipating.

We sat in a lay by just outside Lossiemouth, watching the planes take off and land and the multitude of operations that need to happen in order for the base to function; it was like watching an ant colony.

CHAPTER 14

It's always busy
on a Wednesday!

During the early planning stages of the run, I always
knew that this stretch was going to be hard. Thankfully,
I had my Mum with me as a driver as I needed someone
who would know me and be able to talk to me when
things got really bad. I am not usually negative about
things, but I set off in the wrong mind set. I should have
set off thinking that I was going to beat the road and
that my strength of mind and body would prevail, but
I didn't. From the very first steps on the road, I was
thinking about the pain of the climbs and the loneliness
of the road.

The route went from Elgin and came away from the
coastline for the first time while on the run and ended
in Inverurie. The entire day was spent away from the
coast on small country roads with little scenery other
than a few small hills. I tried to run hard like the
previous day, but no matter how hard I pushed, the
road seemed to beat me. The weather had turned from
a crisp Scottish sunshine to dark and dismal, depressing

rain. Soaked to the bone, I carried on, but with each step a little bit more confidence was eaten away. Soon my negativity and pessimism was turning to anger and frustration. I made it to lunch, but by then pain was dragging me down; I could feel myself becoming more irritable and shutting down from everything. I wasn't answering the phone or reading texts. To top off an already rubbish day, my headphones stopped working, no doubt due to the volume of water that had gone through them during the day – brilliant! Tired, soaked and thoroughly annoyed, I carried on. I talked to myself a lot, singing old rugby songs and at one point, tried to sing as many national anthems as I could remember; the words were always wrong, but I could usually hum a verse or two.

It got to three thirty in the afternoon when the pain in my ankle went from being uncomfortable to almost unbearable. The swelling grew rapidly, until my size 10 trainer became tight to nearly bursting. I stopped and jumped in the van. My fingers were numb with the cold and my ankle was agony. I cut through the laces with a bread knife to get my trainer off, as moving my foot around to wiggle the sodden trainer off my foot was not an option. I still had 17 miles to complete my day and at this point, I just couldn't see it happening at all. I knew the day when my feet swelled would come and had planned for it by having trainers in sizes 10, 10.5, 11 and 11.5. The 11's were unleashed from the box. I winced in pain as I pushed my foot into the brand new (but thankfully dry) trainers. I looked at my Mum who knew I was hurting. "It's just another day, Sam," she said. I could feel tears building and my voice, which is usually deep and direct, was breaking and drifting off towards the end of my sentences.

Stepping back onto the tarmac when you have been in the relative warmth of the campervan is hard, but doing it when everything in your body is screaming for you to stop and rest is even harder. I stumbled into Inverurie a broken man. I needed food and I needed a bed. Nothing had prepared me for this.

Families are a great thing. I think a lot of people take them for granted and I know that a lot of the time I have done the same. I can safely say that if it wasn't for my Mum been there in Scotland on that day, I would not have made it. Thank you Mum, just in case I forget to say this somewhere else. Not only was she there when I was broken, but she was there to make me laugh.

I was annoyed at myself for how I had behaved and acted the previous day. I was like a spoilt brat! I knew it wasn't going to be easy; indeed, nothing in life worth fighting for is ever easy!! I had to get up and crack on, no matter how much it hurt.

Fuelled by anger and some of the best poached eggs on the entire run, I blasted out of the blocks. The rain had not relented overnight and if anything, Scotland was giving me its best! It was doing everything it could to make me quit, but it wasn't going to be today. The swelling had gone down a touch on my ankle overnight, but I remained in the size 11's for the day as the strapping was pretty thick. I was back on the coast again and back breathing in some fresh sea air. Something else which helped spur me on was knowing that I was now heading south. This was the first time in 2 weeks that I had been running south, and it made a huge difference to my mental state.

We stopped for a break at a small isolated beach which would have been quite beautiful had the sun been shining. No houses or people for miles around. I decided to show the people supporting me on the various different social networks that I might be a bit down, but I was not broken! A quick dip in the sea was required! With my mum acting as camera woman, I ran down to the sea in my running tights and dived straight in, the water so cold I couldn't catch my breath, but the feeling was amazing. In fact, the salt water actually helped heal my feet where my nails were missing and the temperature of the water helped cool my muscles, so the rest of the afternoon's running was almost pleasant. I could almost say that from that afternoon came two of the funniest moments of the run.

Firstly, the chemical toilet needed emptying. This to the average camper might sound easy, but I couldn't even work out how to undo the lid. Luckily, I had enough sense to be stood outside the campervan at the time while trying to empty it. I imagine now that I looked like one of the people whose rifle didn't work and so they look straight down the barrel to see of its blocked! I was luckily not using a rifle; I simply held the toilet up, looking for a catch or switch. I can tell already you are thinking, "Wow, this guy is stupid," and yes, when I have come to explain it, I do feel like an idiot. I finally found the catch on the side of the toilet that I thought would release the bottom; it didn't! As I started to look for another switch, I must have pressed a button with my hand which released the bottom of the toilet, the contents of which then hit the floor soaking my leg and filling my trainer. My Mother, who had been near to tears of laughter the whole time, was now in fits of hysterics. My brother, with almost comedic timing, then called and asked how I was getting on. As I scraped the brown and blue sludge off my legs and trainers, I tried to talk to my brother while I laughed at my mother's inability to function, as the laughter was just too much. I quickly stripped at the side of the road, standing in just my boxer shorts, filling a bin liner with my clothes and trainers and discarding them in the nearby bin.

The second amusing incident was not that amusing when it happened, but is now one the best stories to come out of the run. It was late on in the day and I had about 15 miles left to run. We entered Montrose which, going by size of previous towns I had passed through, was quite big and quite busy. I pulled to one side and asked Mum to carry on in the campervan through the town and I would catch her on the other side, otherwise we would have been holding up too much traffic. The campervan drove off into the distance and, as soon as it was out of sight, the heavens opened. Rain drops splashed the tarmac and puddles appeared in a matter of seconds; it felt like I had been hit by a tidal wave, I was so wet. My pace through the town was fast, avoiding traffic and pedestrians as they scurried along the pavement trying to out run the rain. I pushed a good pace right through the centre of the town, always following signs for Arbroath which was my stop at the end of this day. It wasn't too much further, only about 10 miles, but the extra weight that the rain was creating meant I had to work much harder to maintain a good pace. I had been running for about 10 minutes when I started to come out of the other side on Montrose and began a large climb. The rain was coming down so heavily, it had created fast flowing streams in the road gullies. Each step was met with a shoot of cold water up the inside of my leg that almost took my breath away. I started to wonder where Mum would have parked. I had been looking out for her the whole time, as there were ample places to have pulled in on the way out of Montrose, but I thought to myself that she was maybe trying to push me a bit harder to try and get those last few miles hammered out. I reached the peak of the climb after one and half miles running and could see at least a mile into the distance. It was about this time I started to wonder where Mum had pulled over. I carried on running, but rang her just to make sure she had parked up.

"Mum, where have you parked, because I haven't seen you and I have come though Montrose and way out the other side; in fact, I'm not too far from Arbroath?" This is toned down as I was very cold and wet by this point.

"I'm just in a car park where I pulled in about 2 minutes after I left you; I was just reading the paper," she said, amazed that she hadn't seen me.

"You were reading the bloody paper!" I barked with steam coming out of my ears!

"Sorry, I thought you might be a bit longer; I did look every now and again," said Mum, who by this time was laughing too hard to even get any sort of answer out of her.

Mum met up with me 4 miles out of Montrose on a very cold, wet and miserable moor land. It was horrible. Now, when I ask my Mum to join me somewhere, we have an exact location, and there is certainly no paper reading involved!

CHAPTER 15

Breaking the run down

I stopped in a great B&B Arbroath which we found after searching the plethora of one way streets around the town. It was great to stop there, as it's a military town with a base very close to the town. I enjoyed stopping in military towns. I don't know whether it was because they appreciated what I was doing more, or because I felt like I was making a difference to that town, but it always felt better.

The day had started off quite funnily as my Mum reversed the van into a bollard. I told her the dint was not massive, but on closer inspection, it was certainly large enough!

The rain that had begun the previous evening and shown no sign of relenting persisted, but I felt good and so shot out of the door and pushed hard. I broke the day down into sections running two sections of 13 miles in the morning and breaking the afternoon down in to three sections of 7 miles. This way it meant that I just had a small section at the end of the day where I could plod in and would almost be winding down by the time I came to a stop.

There were quite a few highlights in Scotland and one of them was most definitely St Andrews. Not just because of the amazing golf course, but the town itself was beautiful. I ran through a little slower than I normally would through a town or city and really tried to take it all in – the architecture, the smells and the generous people. It was fantastic. To top off an amazing town, my route took me along a coastline which was truly stunning.

Indeed, Scotland had been a stunning place to run through and, to all people who have never been, please go. Stand there and just take in some of the greatest scenes on the planet. I am not saying run round it but, the fresh air certainly makes a difference up there. One thing that made a difference to me was having someone to talk to. On the way down to Leven, I met a woman who was out cycling for the day, but was coming towards the end of her route. She had about 13 miles to go, though at the time, I had no idea. We started chatting and I began to tell my tale of how I had come to be on this rural country road. We talked about anything and everything. She had lived in Scotland her entire life and told me all about the life. It was brilliant; I could have talked to her all day. It makes me sad now that I never got her name. If you are reading this, get in touch. You made my day fly by and I never even said, "Thank you!"

Alone again, I hammered the tarmac. With Bruce Springsteen blasting through my ears, there was nothing I couldn't do! It was funny how an American singer, singing about the USA, could push me so hard to run faster. Thank you to 'The Boss'.

I pushed hard out of Leven, the legs starting to get used to the battering, or maybe I had finally hit on the plan right. Whatever it was, I felt great. I had even run 2 miles in the wrong direction as my new driver (Louisa) was having a small problem with her left and her right! Mum had gone home the previous evening and a friend from work had come to replace her. It wasn't a great start, but nothing seemed to faze me – I just shrugged my shoulders and got the miles back. The sun was shining (that's right people, there is sun in Scotland) and it was baking my back as I sped along towards the capital.

It was strange heading towards Edinburgh as the roads were getting busier and busier. I thought back to just a week earlier where I had hardly seen any civilization at all. It was going to be like this for a while, I thought to myself.

As I mentioned in the first couple of chapters, I am very scared of heights. I know that people think "Oh, me too," but my fear is quite severe. In fact, I get scared on the second rung of a ladder. Entering Edinburgh was a massive problem for me as this involved crossing the Forth Bridge, something that had been on my mind since Glasgow and crossing the Erksine Bridge. I wanted to try and convey my fear to the people at home who were following me on the different sites. Unfortunately, I could not film me on the bridge as I couldn't let go of the hand rail. Eyes tightly shut, I slowly edged across the bridge.

Across the bridge and back on solid ground, I swept through the streets of Edinburgh, running the same street that the marathon takes in. The Edinburgh marathon would be run the day after I completed my last leg into Skipton. That seemed like an eternity away.

I was still running in my tights as I always had, but I had stripped down to a vest it was so warm. It was great to see people on the streets, many of whom cheered me when they saw what I was doing. There was the odd one who looked at me like I was mad, and in all fairness, they could be right! The streets of Edinburgh were great to run – quite flat down along the coastline with beautiful buildings and the occasional view across the capital. It was a fantastic day to run.

On previous days when it had rained, I had never really realised the amount I was sweating. I knew it would still be quite a bit, but nothing makes it more clear to you than when you run in the heat. Sweat poured out of me at one point almost as a constant flow. I knew I needed to take on liquid, but the funny thing was I just didn't feel thirsty. I felt fine, but I had done enough ready and watched enough of Bear Ghrylls to know that water would be my downfall if I didn't keep hydrated. I mixed half an isotonic drink with a pint of water and forced it down my neck. The result was me being sick on the side of the road. Not everything had come back out, so instead of stopping and taking in massive quantities at once, I sipped a little every 10 or 20 minutes. Even that was hard!

CHAPTER *16*

Pride

St George…England….Home. It really is true, there's no place like home! Running south, down the coast and out of Scotland I was almost sad to be leaving. It had been 2 weeks of brutal running, but I wouldn't have changed it. Scotland made the run 'epic'; the blood, the sweat and the tears are on Scotland's tarmac. It's strange to think that I have left body parts in Scotland; indeed, my toe nails will be there for a while I think. Scotland had given me its best. I had prevailed, but the challenge was most definitely still ahead of me. I still had all of England to run and a torturous last week through Wales. Not even half way round, the enormity of what was still to come began to catch up with me.

People at home, and all over for that matter, still doubted me. I know I had proved to some that I was strong enough, but the more pessimistic amongst them still doubted and would always say:

"Well, he has done ok, but he is not even half way yet!"

Keep doubting, I thought to myself. Keep doubting, because I am running, and I am running hard!

I was heading down the east coast now, a strange feeling to think the next time I change direction, I would be running west along the south coast and towards Land's End. I was trying to not get too far ahead of myself, but I also wanted to set realistic goals.

When I ran into Scotland at Gretna, it was great as there were flags and signs to show that you had arrived in Scotland. Entering England was a little bit of anti-climax. We stopped at the layby on the border and had a brew; well, it was just about what you call a brew – actually dishwater might have been a more appropriate title – nevertheless, I was in England.

Pain was again back with a vengeance and hit my knees hard. I headed out after a lunch stop and my body would not relax. Usually the first mile after any stop was hard, but this was something different; this hurt! My knee was burning through the sides and aching at the front. I knew that I didn't have a long time to run, so painful running it would have to be.

My nightly ritual of ice bath, hot bath, food, website update, ice limbs again and sleep prevailed. You will notice the first part of this is the dreaded ice bath. I had started the run by saying that I would never do these, but this was something that became as important to me as food and water. There is no easy way to describe the torture of an ice bath. The minute you touch the water, you begin to make noises resembling a dying sea lion as the breath departs your lungs and areas of your body shrink rapidly! All this torture lasts for approximately 15 minutes, after which my body has shut down and my feet and hands hurt! The difference made by the ice bath was massive; it meant that my muscles had a small amount of recovery time. I decided to show the people of the internet how torturous these were. I think it made for great watching!

The road is an unforgiving place when you are out running by yourself. Even with a driver that will talk to you all the time, it's hard. I did everything to keep my mind busy, but sometimes pain was so constant and so intense that I wasn't able to beat it. I tried to tell myself all the time that I am mentally strong; I repeated things to myself all the time. Run, walk or crawl. Run, walk or crawl. Run, walk or crawl. Run, walk or crawl. Run, walk or crawl. Run, walk or crawl. Run, walk or crawl. Run, walk or crawl. Run, walk or crawl. Run, walk or crawl. Run, walk or crawl. Run, walk or crawl. Run, walk or crawl. Run, walk or crawl. Run, walk or crawl. Run, walk or crawl. Run, walk or crawl. Run, walk or crawl. Run, walk or crawl. Right now it was a crawl – and a slow one at that.

I gave in for an hour and saw a physio. I was lucky that he was able to see me. I had started to believe that physios were somewhere between miracle workers and sadistic torturers. My muscles screamed, my bones creaked and joints made noises that I have never heard since, and will hopefully not hear again until I am quite a lot older. There was now a lump on the front of my knee, pulled forward from the tendons. It was suggested that I stop, but this was just never going to be an option.

Gayle Sharp was an avid supporter of mine throughout the run. I feel it's quite important that I mention Gayle.

Gayle has a family and works full time at the local hospital in the ICU. Even with all her commitments, she supported me every day. Her faith in me was never questioned; it was for people like Gayle that I kept going even when the pain was severe. Gayle texted me at the end of the day with another reminder of why I was running, but she also told me that there was a lot happening back at home to support me when I returned. The idea that I would not return on my planned day never entered her mind; Gayle knew I would finish. I have thanked many people as a group, but you deserve your own mention, Gayle. Thank you! You are an inspiration for working women everywhere and I am proud to say I know you.

Although the day was particularly tough, the running itself was not that hard. It was relatively flat and I was able to run all the way out Holy Island. The last time I went there I was 9 when we went on a school trip. Holy Island is cut off from the mainland at high tide, so I was lucky that I was able to run out there. The return leg was a little bit scarier as the rain grew heavier and the tide was due in. There is nothing like the fear of drowning to make someone speed up!

I still enjoyed arriving at Bed and Breakfasts and looking at the owner's face when I explained to them what I was doing. It was usually a face of complete disbelief and then they would see the van and look at the ever growing ginger beard. The face changed from disbelief to an almost sympathetic smile.

To run with someone is always better than running alone. For those among who are thinking they like solitude, I agree, but once you have run for 20 days and there has been hardly anyone to talk to, you soon change your mind. I was contacted by Tony a few days earlier and he asked if he could run with me. I was nervous as I thought it might affect my pace, or even that we might not get on. All I can say is just talk to Tony. Tony has probably the most infectious personality I have ever met. Running with him was easy as the miles and conversation drifted by, and by the time we had chatted for a few hours, we had already knocked off our first marathon.

Tony is known as 'Tony the Fridge', the reason for this being that when he runs, he runs with a 6 stone fridge on his back to raise money for charities. Thankfully, he didn't bring the fridge for the 50 miles we did. I had spent so long on the road almost talking to myself that I just wanted to be talked at. Tony did just that. It's amazing the things you tell a relative stranger! We shared some of our hardest life stories which all made for a great day. Even running down one of the busiest duel carriage ways in the Newcastle area couldn't stop us. Since finishing the run, Tony has done a number of challenges with the fridge including running 30 Great North Runs, day after day.

Tony is a native of Newcastle, and just like me with Yorkshire, he knows the area like the back of his hand. We ran a route that was not the exact planned route, but one on which I was able to take in all the sights and sounds that the city had to offer. There was one point where even Tony was surprised. A young man – who can only be described as a 'chav' – sauntered up to us with the swagger and cockiness that only a 'chav' can muster:

"Is it you that's doing that run?" he barked, in almost unfathomable English.

"Yeah" I said nervously, making myself as large as possibly.

I could see that even Tony was wary of the guy. He went on to explain that he had been following the run and told us about his family and what it meant to him that some-one was doing something to help our wounded soldiers. His parting gift was to donate £10 to the charity. It will always teach me not to judge a book by its cover.

The morning had come and gone in a flash; the weather had been good and we ran the majority of the day in skins. We stopped for a break and a quick bite to eat and while we were stopped, the clouds gathered. Within one hour, we had gone from blazing sun shine to monsoon rain. Thankfully, the rain was not cold, but it was heavy. We pushed out along the sea front making our way along the coast towards Middleborough. Tony did everything he could to keep my spirits up. We changed clothes a few times, stripping down to light weight running gear.

Tony asked me questions all day about how I planned the run and what I was doing at night. I told him that we were just driving into the town after 50 miles, then looking round for somewhere to stay. "That's just insane," he said, in complete amazement that this was what I had been doing for the last 20 days. "Don't worry about hotels anymore, I'll get my guys on it." said Tony. This is how it was for the rest of the run. Tony would call me every day and ask where I would be finishing and I would tell him the name of the town, and my hotel would be ready and waiting when I arrived. The only problem with this was cost. Hotels are expensive, especially when you spend 50 nights in them. At this point, I should thank Matt Morrison; Matt spent every day haggling with Hotel owners to get us the best deal, so a massive thank you, Matt.

The first hotel he sorted out was one I will never forget. It was called *The Gables* and their main pull for customers was that the husband and wife team who ran the hotel performed folk music duets. There is not much you can say when someone has booked a hotel for you, but I can safely say it wouldn't be my first choice; but beggars can't be choosers, as they say. Tony and I said our good-byes and I made my way to the hotel. The front door was locked with hardly any sign of life, so I walked round the back and opened the door. All I could think of was that I should have rung my Mum and said, "If you don't hear from again, I have been murdered! However, I was given a friendly North-east welcome and shown to my room where I went to make a cup of tea; the biscuits went out of date the previous year, the water was a browny-green colour and the shower looked like they had been dipping sheep in it. I got changed and went to bed, praying for morning.

CHAPTER 17

The Green,
Green Grass of Home

I had been looking forward to this day since turning South in Elgin. I was finally setting foot back in Yorkshire, and I couldn't wait to breathe some Yorkshire air! I was coming down from Redcar and ending in Filey, but it was going to be tough. The rubbish night's sleep had not helped either, but I was still feeling good from my day with Tony. I wanted people to see me out on the road where I wanted people to accompany me, either running or cycling, so they could see what it was like for me.

The hardest thing about running certain areas was that I knew what was coming. I had visited Whitby before and I knew that it was going to be hard. By now, downhill was hurting me much more than anything else. The pressure of my body weight pushing through my joints was agony. Tom, my driver from Scotland, had come back out to the coast to visit his girlfriend's family. He was dropped off with his mountain bike and stayed with me for half a day. Tom was great! He doesn't know how to be negative and sees no bad in anyone, so it was always good to talk to him. We had spent some of the toughest days on the run together and he knew when I was hurting and when I needed someone. I was happy to see him!

Tom and I attacked the hills and pushed hard across the unforgiving moorlands until we hit Scarborough. The roads were busy, so I felt compelled to keep moving at a decent pace or people might have accused me of walking it. This type of attitude played often on my mind. I wanted to make sure people always saw me running, so they couldn't claim that what I was doing was easy.

By this point of the run, I had come to appreciate different types of tarmac. Many people might just look at a road and think, "Yeah, it's a road," but for me there were certain types of road that made a difference. Certain tarmacs were easier to run on than others. Heavy tarmac, with big pieces of stone in, were more draining to run on because it felt like I was having to push harder to get more out of the road. Smooth roads were my favourite – the types of tarmac that had been melted or worn down and looked smooth and shiny. These were the best. I glided along and could feel the effort I was expelling into the road being bounced back through my trainers.

A famous endurance runner always signs off his emails or letters with 'may the wind always be at your back'. I now understand why that is so important. Head wind and tail winds over 50 miles have made the difference between 11 hours running or 13 hours running. The effort that is extorted to run into a head wind is massive, meaning that more calories are consumed. For the majority of the day, the wind was at my back. I had to come quite a way in land as I needed to cross the Humber Bridge. The Humber Bridge is not as scary as the other bridges I have crossed as it's very solid and has a nice wide path to run or cycle along. An added bonus is that you can't see through the floor, only getting an idea of its height by peering over the edge which is something I would never do!

I met a group of runners at the south side of the Humber Bridge and they continued with me for the last section of the day. It was like being back with Tony. They told me about themselves and how they had come to see what I was doing. They asked me questions about my diet, sleeping patterns and my training leading up to the run. In return, they showed me the sights of the East Riding of Yorkshire. We ran through sleepy little villages called Barton and Barrow as we traversed our way down the coastline to Immingham.

My shin was burning and I started to panic that I might be getting shin splints. This would have been a nightmare. I have never had them, but I have spoken to other people about them and they tell me they are agony. I have always thought that my legs would do whatever I told them to do, but doubt was slowly creepy back into my mind; this could be the end. However, I bottled this up and didn't mention the pain to anyone, though it was there and people knew it.

Making into Immingham was a great feeling. For a strange reason I was starving today. I needed to eat badly. I am good at eating. 2 starters, 2 mains and 2 puddings were beginning to be my every-day staple diet. I needed to consume the calories in an evening, as I was struggling to keep food down during the day. I never felt hungry during the day, but that night I could have carried on eating and eating.

CHAPTER 18

Flat does not mean easy

My body was feeling every year of my twenty-nine years by this point. Many of my old rugby injuries were pushing through and hurting me.

Lincolnshire is known for being flat, but it is something else entirely to see it and run through it. Just massive, wide open spaces where you can see for miles. It's completely opposite to the rolling hills of the Yorkshire Dales, but at the same time, beautiful in its own right. The flat lands, although bursting with fields of crops, bring with them an entirely new challenge – head wind. The wind and rain in Lincolnshire were enough to take the skin off your face. Relentless rain battered me from top to bottom, soaking me down to my boxers.

On day 24, it didn't matter what the heavens had in store for me. It was going to be a good day. Friends and family arrived from home, and never in my life had I been so happy to see people. People surrounded me as I ran, some running two or three miles, others running 16!! Every step they took with me made mine easier.

Matt, the guy who had originally planned to run with me, spent the entire day next to me on a bike. He looked like the Michelin Man with the amount of layers he had on, but not one moan came from him. I knew he was cold and I knew that 50 miles on a bike and 5 miles an hour was hard, but he supported me all day. I ran much harder than normal, maybe in a vain attempt to show my friends and family that I was holding up well, but also it felt easier with these people around me.

Calling in at a Little Chef for dinner, I am sure the waitress has seen many sights, but not many would have topped ours. Seven people, all soaked to the skin, me still in my running tights and skin top. Steam rose off the table as we entered the warm room from the cold. Cakes, pastries, potatoes and pasta covered the table. How many calories were consumed at the table is anyone's guess, but I am pretty sure that feeding time at the zoo is more civilized!

As after most torrential down pours, the next day tends to be a little milder. This was certainly the case. The East Coast was proving to be a much more beautiful experience that originally anticipated. In truth, I had not known what to expect – maybe washed up and desolate seaside towns – but that wasn't really the case. All the towns along the East Coast were busy and vibrant, with many making the most of what they had. In a way, this kind of sums up Britain. We can't offer the greatest weather, or even the most amazing mountains, but we make the most of what our little island has to offer.

Cromer is a town that I have never visited or really heard much about, but it is certainly a place I would visit again.

It's a sleepy town, the type you see on TV and think, "Awwww, I would love to live there." Lined with different coloured beach houses and gorgeous Bed and Breakfasts, Cromer is beautiful.

All the way from Kings Lynn to Cromer was run in a vest and running tights. Not a single time in the previous 24 days had I been able to wear less than si6 layers of clothing, so wearing a vest was something of a luxury. Unfortunately, due to being one of the whitest men on the face of the planet, I can burn during a cold day in February! But my skin had held up pretty well. By the end of the day, I did have tan lines where my vest had been, but luckily for me, they were not sore. I imagine sun burn would not be pleasant while trying to run.

I always say to people when I am trying to motivate them in the gym, "Well done, you are half way, just the same to do again." Actually feeling that is something else. The feeling of been half way was an amazing feeling. It was around this time the doubters began to change their tune. They knew I was for real, that with every step I was pushing towards home and towards my finish line.

Norfolk, Essex and Suffolk were passing by and I even managed to sneak a quick physio appointment with ex-England cricketer Neil Foster, a reasonably strange encounter due to the location, but one that was desperately needed. Like many other doctors and physios, Neil knew I needed to stop, but also knew that this wasn't happening. The running had been good, flat land with good tarmac and reasonable weather. As with the rest of the run, the rain had followed and as Britain was enduring its driest April and May for 50 years, I was being hailed as the answer to the drought. Wherever I ran, the rain soon followed.

Your mind can wander a lot while you run, and like many people, I used to use running as a way to clear my head. I had now been running for 27 days. My head was clear, in fact, the few thoughts I did have were few and far between and usually involved food, or where to stop for the toilet. It's how I imagine being hypnotized feels like – I was in a constant trance. I didn't know who people were and what they were doing. I would just stare at the road and look at my feet. The noise of my trainers against the tarmac was metronomic and gave me a rhythm that would beat through my mind. You might have had this feeling before on a train, or even when driving when you can't remember the past 5 or 10 miles and you wonder to yourself how you managed to get to the place you are. Instead of this being 5 or 10 minutes I would spend days like this. Described as vacant and emotionless, I find it hard now to describe the days to you as the only parts I can truly recall are where I would stop for a break and I would break out of the trance. Although, strangely, I can recall odd things that come back to me, like a simple smell, which will always ignite memories. A prime example of this is the pig farms of Suffolk. Suffolk, I believe, could quite possibly have more pigs than humans per square foot! Every time I go near a pig farm now, the memories of the Suffolk coast come screaming back to me. Small lanes winding along with farms either side, or pigs as far as the eye could see!

Pushing on past day 25 and up towards 30, I could see that 'Epic Run Fever' was growing at home. The messages were a lot more frequent and the websites were filling up with people trying to contact me. It was a fantastic feeling and one that pushed me harder to complete each day. No matter who the driver was, or where I was, we always wanted to get the day finished so we could see the websites and look at the donations. 'Epic Run Fever' – Wow, I had never known that something as simple as running could create something so amazing that it could bring together an entire community.

The campervan/support vehicle/kitchen/toilet/wind break/ emergency vehicle had done great so far and running repairs had been at a minimum. Unfortunately, the fuel gauge that had not worked for the entire trip was still not working and our estimations must have been somewhat off. It had just turned 4.30 in the afternoon with the weather, for once, being kind – the sun shining. The van had tootled along and we were about 7 miles off finishing for the day when, with a splutter and a fart, we came to a grinding holt. I had not noticed that the van was no longer behind me until I was a further 200 feet down the road. A few turns of the key and we knew that there was something not quite right. I rang a friend who told me to try a few different things, but as he was 500 miles away and my mechanical expertise finished at where to put windscreen wash, I knew we needed a garage. This is where the brilliance of modern technology saved the run. A quick look on my phone suggested that there was a garage within a mile of where we were. One phone call to them and an explanation of what we were doing and a vehicle arrived with a tank of fuel. I still to this day can't remember his name, or even the name of the fuel station, but if you ever read this, thank you!

CHAPTER 19

A Sheep and two lambs

The support I received while I ran was one of the most amazing things I have witnessed, but what happened during days 28 to 30 were just astonishing! I think I might be one of the only people who has ever received a donation of a sheep and 2 lambs!! Now that is what you call a donation! This was all done through the auction. As I stated right at the start, people from Yorkshire have a certain mentality and I know that these sheep and lambs will have meant a lot to that farmer.

Running along ancient roads and along the White Cliffs of Dover were amazingly special. To any British person, I believe that these represent part of Britain's identity and heritage. It was a humbling experience to stand on the cliffs and look out over the water.

I had been running for 30 days, so a month had passed; it was strange to think the things that had happened while I had been away at home. For many, life will have passed by normally. For me, it felt like years since I had seen my family and friends. It was hard not to feel some sadness, but at the same time, also think of the people that were out in different parts of the world fighting to maintain our freedom, many of whom don't see friends and family for months at a time.

I tried hard all the time to keep myself motivated and keep my mind on track. Even now, people ask me how I did it. One way was finding playlists on my I-pod that I didn't mind listening to over and over again. Call it sad, call it whatever you like, but the *Rocky Soundtrack* makes my hair stand on end. If I hear *Eye of the Tiger* while I am at home, I will leap up and feel super pumped and ready to beast my body!! Unfortunately, my body had already taken the battering of a lifetime and there was not much more beating it could take.

Music was not my only motivation, nor was it the main one. Every so often, I would get a message that would stop me in my tracks and just let me know how lucky I really was. I had done a lot of radio interviews for BFBS which is the forces radio station. Someone had heard me on there and decided to get in contact. He was soldier whose best friend had lost both his legs while in Afghanistan. He told me of the amazing care he received while he was in Camp Bastion and the care he received when he got home. He echoed a thousand texts I had already had, that without people like Help for Heroes, his friend would be left without a hope. It is my opinion, that there is not much more to evoke human emotion than listening, or seeing the struggle of another human who can overcome the odds. This I feel was exactly what the run had become. One person overcoming the odds.

Bruised and battered, I travelled through Folkestone and, while on the sea front, ran into a small welcoming committee. A flag waved in the distance with a small group gathered round. As I neared the flag, it became clear it was a H4H flag. Three children stood in the bleakest Folkestone breeze to have a photo taken with me. Cold and wet, we stood and posed for our photograph. It puts a massive smile on your face knowing someone would come and support you in such horrific conditions. We sat a mile further up the beach and had a warm drink, my fingers thawing, as I grasped the polystyrene cup so hard, it spilled several times.

I had traversed the outer edges of the capital, sprinted across the Dartford Crossing, weaved my way through Margate and Ramsgate around the coast, but one major highlight for this 'uber geek' was to be able to have a sandwich in a town called Sandwich!! Sat on a rock in the middle of the town car park with my Sandwich, completely at ease, I wondered if things could get much better? I was three weeks from home and it was not the fear of failure that laid heavy on me now, as I now knew my legs could carry me that far. My fear now was tripping up and injuring myself, or being at the mercy of something that was out of my control.

CHAPTER 20

Other people run too!

"People sometimes sneer at those who run every day, claiming they'll go to any length to live longer. But don't think that's the reason most people run. Most runners run not because they want to live longer, but because they want to live life to the fullest. If you're going to while away the years, it's far better to live them with clear goals and fully alive then in a fog, and I believe running helps you to do that. Exerting yourself to the fullest within your individual limits: that's the essence of running, and a metaphor for life – and for me, for writing as whole. I believe many runners would agree"
— Haruki Murakami, *What I Talk About When I Talk About Running*

"Every morning in Africa, a gazelle wakes up, it knows it must outrun the fastest lion or it will be killed. Every morning in Africa, a lion wakes up. It knows it must run faster than the slowest gazelle, or it will starve. It doesn't matter whether you're the lion or a gazelle-when the sun comes up, you'd better be running."
— Christopher McDougall, *Born to Run: A Hidden Tribe, Superathletes, and the Greatest Race the World Has Never Seen*

Day 32, one of the toughest on the run, but also one of the best. I felt that I needed something to help me kick start my day; I needed someone to know how I was feeling, but, in reality, nobody could. All the messages in the world couldn't seem to shake me out of this mood, so I grabbed my phone and decided to google 'Quotes about running'. These two quotes stuck out amongst a sea of others. I feel like the lion and the gazelle: I know every morning I have to get up, I won't starve, but I will fail and, for me, that just wasn't an option. GET UP AND MOVE!

Head down and crack on, remember your roots, remember why you are running and burn your legs, like they have never burnt. Go to war with the road and beat it; with every hill, and every single step, push harder and harder to make the run submit. Waging war against anything and everything was the only way I was going to complete the run. Forget the pain, forget everything you think you know about running, push through it; nothing worth doing is ever easy.

There is something in Britain called the North, South divide. People in the North are believed to be stingy, hard fisted, gritty, but friendly people. Whereas people in the south are hostile, unfriendly people that only care about themselves – apparently. If you believe this, you're an idiot. I can argue that every single town I went through showed, in its own way, that there are amazing communities all over that are just bursting to show their generosity.

I drafted in emergency drivers on day 32. People who had no idea who I was, or where I was from, but knowing who I was running for, wanted to help. Mayday calls were put out all over the nation to try and help the Epic Runner. They came in their hundreds to help and it was something I will never forget to my dying day. People volunteering their time to come and drive for me. People willing to drive thousands of miles just to drive 50 miles with me at 5 miles per hour. Wow!

One person I was able to meet while I was running was Liz Leighton, the sister of a lady who comes in the gym I work at. A tenuous link, but one I have to say I am glad I had. Liz arranged for me and my family to visit HMS Dragon and sit on the Captain's Chair. A great way to take a break from running on what had turned out to be a pretty dismal day. Meeting the personnel on board and watching their faces when I told them what I was doing, was classic, I wish I had taken a picture of all of them. Each one in turn trying to fathom just how far 50 miles is and then trying to work out 50 days of it. Watching as the penny dropped, "So you're doing 2500 miles?"

"Yeah, I am," I replied with a wry smile, as it was something I had heard for the past 32 days. It felt good to receive their gratitude, undoubtedly all of them serving on board that ship had known someone injured, or had a link to someone that had been. The ship itself will, at some point in the future, be used to help in our war on terrorism.

Not only was it arranged for me to visit HMS Dragon, but I would staying with Liz in Waterlooville that evening and heading out from their in the morning, meeting up with some more emergency drivers. A nice, comfy bed and a great ice bath – absolutely brilliant!

CHAPTER 21

They think it's all over.....

It's strange to think that entire run nearly came crashing down due to me being locked in a bedroom!! Out of bed at 6am, I went to get out of the room and pulled the handle off the door!! Maybe I didn't know my own strength! With the latch broken, the door handle was useless. What's worse, I was on the top floor of the house and could not be heard. I sat for a while contemplating what to do when Liz arrived with a cup of tea. Due to the broken latch, I was still stuck! Liz tried a number of different kitchen utensils and screwdrivers to try and get the door open, but the option of jumping out the third story window was looking more and more like the only option. Another problem was my bladder! Like many people, I don't always get up when I need the toilet right away and choose to stay cosy and warm for a few more minutes, knowing that when I get up, I can go straight to the bathroom. Today this had been plan, so my bladder was full and about to burst, and I was stuck. Luckily, Liz has some very nice neighbours who came with a full tool box, and 20 minutes later, I was out and straight into the bathroom. It's always difficult meeting people for the first time when bursting for a wee! You don't want to seem rude, but know that if they don't move soon, they're going to be stood in a puddle!

The day was spent running between Christchurch and Bridport on the South Coast. I was running east to west and heading towards Lands End, where I would turn north for the last time and head back home. It was all I could think about, turn right and head north, and I would be heading home. 33 days had passed since Blackpool and the running was certainly not getting any easier. Pain was constant. The old break in my foot grew what felt like inches every day and bore into the roof of my trainer which rubbed the skin off the top of foot.

My driver for the day was Matt, a minister from Poole in Dorset. He knew the area well and even allowed me to spend my first brew break in his beautiful home. He has his own social network following and blogs daily about his exploits. It still astounds me that social networks allowed him to find me and help me when I was in dire need of a driver.

Matt dropped me on Bournemouth beach; if you have never been there, it really is brilliant. The beach path runs along a stretch of sand and is great for running as it's nice and flat. It was 11am and there were plenty of people filling the paths. It was always tough when people saw me without the support vehicle because they didn't know why I was running; they just assumed I was another runner out on a mid-morning run. They didn't know that I had actually just travelled about 1,500 miles to be there and I had been running for the past month – through all conditions – to share this path with them.

The scenery of the beach was soon gone and I was back running through the streets of Poole and Bridport. Once again, people supported me without question; the messages came flocking through in waves as traffic built up behind me, and not a single beep was sounded in anger. Matt left at about the 25 mile mark, as I didn't want him to be too far away from home, so I dropped him at the train station. It's still great to see what people will do to help a good cause. It can bind a country and really shows what people think of you and the cause. I may never see Matt again, but what he did for me will never be forgotten.

The weather was stunning and the running had been good all day. As I ate my dinner, a taxi driver slowly walked up to the van. He asked the usual pleasantries and then told me about his son who had just set off to Afghanistan; he thanked me for what I was doing and, with his parting words, emptied his change from his taxi into my lap. One random act of kindness had once again changed everything. My brief encounter with the taxi driver further instilled my belief that there are good people all over the world, and everyone has the potential to perform a good turn.

It is at this point where I have a small confession to make. I had lied to Matt. I had lied to a minister. I felt guilty about making him come and drive for me when he himself must have had a lot more important things to do. I had got to the half-way point, but my driver was not due to the next evening and I just couldn't ask any more of people. I knew what I was about to was incredibly stupid, but it had to be done. I wouldn't tell anyone – I would just get on and do it. I needed to make sure everyone at home know I was fine, or they would panic. I had to get the van and me the next 75 miles without stopping running. For many, you might say, "Simple – get in and drive it!" This was never going to happen. There was only one way to do it: the caterpillar technique! This is where I would run a certain distance, remember where I was and then get a bus back to the van. I would then drive the van the mileage I had just run, then get out and do that all over again. If you are reading the book, you are the only people who know I did this. I didn't want sympathy, but nor did I want people coming hundreds of miles just to drive for one day, so this is how it was going to be for the next 75 miles.

Buoyed by the generosity of the taxi driver, I loaded a rucksack with everything I would need to run ten miles and set off into the South Coast sun. I figured I would push hard towards Bridport for tonight, so I was running about 9 minute miles. I needed as much rest as possible for the slog tomorrow. Pain burned deep in my right foot and tears ran down my face as I cursed myself for lack of planning. How could I have been so stupid? I then started to ask why I had let Matt go when I needed him!! What an absolute idiot. My anger pushed me harder and I was no longer running at a sustainable pace. The tracker in my ears ticked over the mile at '6 minutes 53 seconds' barked by the woman who tracked the miles. A loud swearword was quickly snapped back at the woman on the end of the App. I had to slow down, but I was burning pure anger, pure adrenalin, and hatred of myself pushed me harder and faster. After 10 miles, I looked for the nearest bus stop. There was a bus due in the next 30 minutes. It was a depressing drive back on the bus, made equally worse by a bus full of people all wondering who this sweaty mess was and why he didn't shave? Not only was the bus ride a torturous journey, the drive back in the camper was just as awful, knowing my tears were still wet on this road. I arrived back at my marker. Donning my rucksack once again, I headed out to complete the last 15 miles in one full section. For the first time in a long time, I began to think I was not going to make it. It was beating me. I was losing. My stomach burnt through the lack of fuel. All I needed to do was to stop and eat, as I had gone too fast for too long – an idiotic mistake to make at this stage. Arriving at the hotel that night was brilliant. They expected me to arrive with all these support medics and hundreds of bags. Instead, I arrived dripping in sweat, a mix of sweat and tears dripped from my face. Just me and my back pack. I asked the receptionist where the nearest bus stop was and got an evening bus back to the camper. Thankfully, the bus was empty. It was about 8.20pm when I finally got into my hotel, where I then had to meet the local media. In the back of my mind was the horror of tomorrow and what that was going to be like.

CHAPTER 22

It's still a long hard slog

It took me a long time to realise that there are no such things as easy miles. By day 34, every mile is tough. If you happen to believe differently, you are a much stronger person than I. I have never really believed much in God and all that shindig, but after day 34, I knew there was a hell, and I had just run through it.

When people ask me about the run now, they always ask what or where was the hardest? I usually say day 2, or Lynmouth, both of which were flipping horrific. I never mention day 34, as this was the day that broke me. It broke me down to my very core. I don't think I have ever, or will ever, feel like that again in my life. The rain battered me from 6am and didn't stop the whole day. This wasn't just a light drizzle either; this was the type of rain that eroded rocks, that washed houses out to sea. These were big, massive rain drops that felt like a punch in the gut when each one landed.

I had barely slept the night before, mainly due to the fact that I finished very late and also because I knew that today I was going to have to run 50 miles unsupported.

I awoke at 4.30am. I had checked with reception the previous night to ensure I was ok to leave early. I must have only had two hours maximum when my alarm broke the silence. Stiff and sore from the previous day, I rolled from the bed and couldn't even manage to get to my feet. Instead, I had to roll onto all fours and slowly lever myself up. I imagine it would have been quite amusing had you been stood next to me, and it was interesting for me to have a quick glimpse into the future to see what I will be like as an old man! Fifteen minutes to put on a sock and the agony was almost unbearable. I was no longer holding in the anguish in a manly, macho way. No – not at all! Right now, I was laid on my bed again screaming at my sock to magically jump on my foot. The couple of hours stolen from my sleep in order to try and get longer on the road were being slowly diminished.

I was afraid that when I started writing this that I would become repetitive and that would run out of ways to describe pain. I don't have that fear now. In fact, all I hope is that from my constant repetition of the words 'ow' and 'agony' you are somehow able to grasp that this was not some tiny jog on the way to find some sort of inner peace. This was a brutal game of 'Mercy'. The road would punish my body; pushing harder and harder to submit, I would respond by pounding the tarmac till my bones shattered. Brutal it was, soul searching and peaceful? You've got to be kidding!

20 miles down and I knew that my body was about done. The rain just wouldn't stop. I don't mind running in the rain usually, I see it as an extra challenge, and generally,

it keeps me cool. On this occasion, the rain was beating me; I could feel myself dropping in pace, morale, and just my general will to keep going. I needed a break, but I still had over two weeks till that was ever going to happen. On the bus back to my van, for the third time that day, I sat and stared blankly out of the window, the only thing I could think of was quitting. This was the bottom; I couldn't feel any lower. I began to run the fourth stretch of ten miles, when I started to feel a bit better. My body had loosened just enough to regain my normal stride pattern and that feeling is like no other. To feel like you can move and run again is brilliant. It had taken something completely stupid and to many people utterly pointless, but I had my stride back! I remember smiling for the first time that day. It felt great to smile again.

CHAPTER 23

The End of England

I had been running for 37 days solid. I had seen every type of rain imaginable to man. I had run to the top of Scotland and to the bottom of England. I was finally heading north and up towards Wales. The feeling of getting to Land's End was incredible; to stand and look out to sea and know you are at the end of the country was incomparable. After a quick pose for a photo, I carried on pushing north. I was back with a driver aiding me and it made all the difference. We pushed hard along the winding roads, with the sun beating down on my back. Running in the sun was still something I was struggling to get used to. I had monitored my fluid intake reasonably well during the wet and cold days which was easy. I would stop and have a cup of tea if my hands were cold, or an isotonic drink to help fuel my muscles for a while. It was strange to change clothes due to excess sweat rather than due to being so heavily saturated with rain. Salt lined my running cap and crystalised on the peak; to anyone wondering whether it was hard work, this was evidence enough!

It was a strange feeling to stand at Lands End and know that so many other journeys had either finished or started on that very ground. The Land's End to John O'Groats challenge is probably one of the most well-ridden and run challenges in Britain every year. I wondered for a while how many tears of joy had been shed on that ground, how many thoughts of fear and trepidation there had been had when people had set out on their own challenges. I waited for a while and stared down the road that has a 'finish' and a 'start' line on it. "Not long," I thought, while some cyclists completed their challenge and fell into the arms of their loved ones. Raw, pure and uncontrollable emotion all over their faces. Not long.

While I was at University, I played a lot of rugby and I was coached by one of the best coaches and one of the hardest men I have ever met. Some of what this guy instilled in me was helping me run now. His name was Kev Greaves, a copper from Merseyside who had a glare that would send a lion running. For those of you au fait with rugby union, kicking the ball is large part of the game, hence why everyone knows Jonny Wilkinson. What Kev did was tell us we were not allowed to kick the ball, ever, even if it meant losing the game. I had wondered for years why were not allowed to kick. What good did it really do? Looking back now, I see exactly what it did. We did everything at 100%; we ran every play, we hit every ruck and we did it all for our coach. We had a fear of failure, not for ourselves, but for Kev. Kev instilled a belief in all of us that we were stronger, fitter, harder and faster than our opposition. That belief still runs hard in my blood. This run was my rugby pitch now and I was pushing hard towards the finish line. Ten minute miles meant for much better running, but (and not to sound big headed) it meant that my days were over quicker which also meant longer time to rest.

CHAPTER 24

Smiling big, running hard and running home

Day 39 was one of my proudest moments on the run and is one that will live long in my memory. I ran into Chivnor Marine Base early on the morning of day 39 where I had arranged to meet some servicemen. After the initial meetings and pleasantries, two of the boys ran with me and we headed off north. I was aided by a friend of a friend from home who had travelled all the way down to see me. He was actually a friend of my Dad's, an old rugby boy, but it was great to have someone else to chat to. Added to the fun that day were my drivers. Paul and Shaun were rugby boys from Skipton. I had played in the same team as these guys for the past 6 years. They were like the chuckle brothers in the van together. Whenever my head dropped or I felt down, they would do something to make me laugh. This could have been anything from a simple toot of the horn to full blown karaoke! With the help of the army boys, donations were amazing; toots and whistles howled out all round the local towns – it was brilliant. You could really see what the base meant to the local town.

After about 10 miles, one of the army boys called it a day. Paul and Shaun ensured they gave him plenty of stick for not running the full 50, but in all fairness, these boys were running in full army fatigues. Then the weather took a turn for the worse, as did the terrain. I had chosen to move inland to collect the boys during the morning which had also meant more climbs, many of which were lung busting, back breakers. I was getting good at judging how hard a climb was by how far I had to lean forward. If I could lean forward and touch the road, it meant it was very steep! The second of the army boys did a full marathon and I don't think he will ever fully appreciate how much those miles meant to me. They had run because we shared a common friend who had been injured while on patrol in Afghanistan. It was great to hear their stories about him and about army life in general. It was something so completely different to how my life was at this point in time.

If you are a non-runner reading this, or even a runner who thinks, that doesn't sound too bad. Go to your local gym, get on the treadmill, stick the gradient at 2% and run for three hours, then up the gradient to 10% and run for an hour. After this, put the gradient up to 15% and run for one more hour. Was it easy? Well, that was half of one of my days and that was only a small gradient as the treadmill usually only goes to 15% and not 25% like some of the gradients I had to contend with. Pushing out of Lynmouth was a 25% gradient and one of the toughest climbs on the entire run. I had always tried to keep my heart rate at a constant beat, so this meant not working too much harder on a climb. The Lynmouth climb completely blew this out of the water! I was shattered and out of breath when I hit the summit. Even the van struggled to get up that climb; I knew it must have been tough. Trying to sustain the regular heart rate proved too much, sweat poured and the further I leant forward, the more it pushed forward into my eyes. Sweat in the eye burns and this in turn made me really agitated, which made for aggressive running. Aggression is the same in running as it is in any sport – when its controlled and harnessed, it can be your greatest ally; when you let aggression control your emotion, you have lost control.

CHAPTER 25

The last 10

I had only ever been to Wales on a school trip when I was about 13, so needless to say, I had absolutely no idea what to expect. I knew that the Welsh were passionate people who were very proud of their heritage and their country. Having run through it, I can see why. It was the most amazing place, with the sea on one side with rolling hills, into the valleys on the other, a breath-taking contrast of lush green grass to long, sandy, almost untouched beaches. The weather was certainly helping me enjoy the Welsh countryside. It wasn't all picturesque beautiful running. I had crossed the Severn Bridge and stayed my first night in the center of Cardiff. Cardiff is a beautiful metropolitan city that doesn't feel like a capital city. It has an almost small town feel to it, with a friendly community vibe comprising a blend of cultures that can be seen from one end of the city to the other. Navigating the city was not easy and a couple of wrong turns were taken quite a few times in Wales. It always seems easy to navigate when you know where you are going, but I had no idea and no map. I would look back at the guys who would then look at each other, look back at me and then shrug! Brilliant, I thought! I am lost,

I am shattered and I have dumb and dumber trying to navigate me round a capital city!

It was interesting when running in the different towns to see how many are the same as others around Britain. I ran into Barry and immediately thought I had run into Barrow-in-Furness back up in Cumbria. Two towns are depending massively on the shipping industry and both towns struggling with the current economic climate. It was one thing that humbled me even more. I was running in a town that was struggling; it had nothing to offer its youth and unemployment was unbelievably high and yet we had more donations, cheers and toots than at any other time during the run. It shows what the run was doing to people and to communities. When people share a common love or goal, they will do whatever they can to try and help. That's what the people of Barry were doing. My face was a face of anguish; they knew that, like the town itself, I too was struggling. Too many climbs in one day and I was broken for the next, as every climb burnt into the soles of my feet. It was the feeling you get if you stand up too long, your feet get really warm and burn with each step. Unlike when this happens in normal life, I couldn't seem to get a break from it. Even when I had a break, I took my trainers off and tried to air my feet, but they still hurt. The 1,000 mile socks were shredded! Stained with blood and sweat, I removed them with a few layers of skin, and the shooting pain returned. The only problem with removing a sock mid run is knowing that I will have to put another pair back on. Reapplying the sock was a millimetre by millimetre operation! Each movement of the aforementioned pulled hard on the broken skin, like sandpaper.

CHAPTER 26

Getting complacent in the sun

I had been running for over 40 days. I was running on empty. If there had been a medic amongst the support people in my vehicle, they would have said that I was massively dehydrated, was losing weight rapidly and needed a rest. I knew my body well by this point and I knew what I had in my tank. My mind was still focused and I knew that I could make it, but my body was starting to crumble under the stress. My right hip and been hurting for a few days and it was only getting worse. I had upped the pain killers, but by this point, they were not even beginning to touch it. Every day I was doing the school boy error of changing my running style; I was doing this to adapt to the pain. I had to adapt. If I didn't, I would have no chance. I can usually tell when my weight fluctuates, and whether it goes up or down, it's usually not by a massive amount. If I weigh too much, I will hit the cardio and cut the bad weight; if I go too light, I will start eating more, cut the cardio out and just focus on heavy lifting. This had been my basic way of keeping my body at a stable rate my entire life. After day 40 when we were well into Wales, I looked down and I could see veins appearing in my stomach. Vascularity is a sure sign of low body fat, and as I had never seen them in my stomach before, I knew things were getting serious.

Wales was still treating me to some awesome scenery and brilliant roads to run on. It was like running on a cricket pitch for the majority of the time. The easy, smooth tarmac was a blessing for me at this point; my knee lift and heel flick were shorter and shorter every day and I was running more and more stiff legged as I ran through Britain's smallest city of St David's out on the coast in Wales. They were not wrong; it is indeed very small and well worthy of this accolade. In this lovely place, the size of some villages, I stopped for a while and had something to eat.

It was amazing to see what difference the attention of one famous person could do for publicity. The comedian and fellow northerner, John Bishop had recently done a grueling sports relief challenge that was shown on national television. The nation saw the effects that the run, cycle and row had on John's body and mind and how he coped with the pain that it caused. Once again, like me, a person who can empathize with pain and anguish. John shared my news with his fans via his social networking sites and within minutes, I had hundreds more people following the run and hundreds more donations on line. This was just what I needed. I needed that boost so badly from the public; it showed me that still, after all this time, people were still willing me to get through and complete the run.

I have spent the majority of this book never really naming anyone in particular, but Sara (my wife) deserves a mention. Sara had been my driver for longer than anyone. She had put up with my whining and moaning for longer than any other person. At this point of the run, I was hurting; I was tired and mentally drained, so I took everything out on her. She sat every day and got me ice, never once moaning or complaining. If you ever decide to do something like this, or indeed any other challenge, surround yourself with the people you love and who love you, because even at your darkest times, they are still there to make you smile. They are still there to tell you that you haven't failed in what you are doing and, in their eyes, you have not let anyone down.

Pain was eating at me like a virus; it was sapping all my emotions as I fought hard to keep pushing through. Each rest point was spent redressing open sores on my feet, re-strapping my knees and ankles and consuming pain killers and anti-inflammatories like they were Smarties. The Welsh hills were beginning to get the better of me; I was beginning to think it might be a few steps too far for me.

I began to end all my blog updates the same way; I was wanting to show the nation and all the new followers that even when you are down, a smile is all it takes to push right on through and come out the other side. I know it sounds very happy clappy and a little bit of motivational babble, but that's all it took. I was running off raw emotion, the only thing keeping me going was the support I was receiving from the people on social network sites and off the public. All I thought was that if a person sees me smiling, they will think, "Wow, look at that guy, he has been running for over 40 days and he can still wave and smile." If people just take the time to smile now, it really can make the difference to your day. My strap line was now, "Smiling Big, Running Hard and Running Home." I loved it; it summed everything up perfectly and was exactly the massage I wanted to get across to people. I would not be beaten and even when a climb was bursting my lungs, I would dig deep, push hard and smile, as I knew that somewhere, something much worse was happening. They say a smile is infectious and that a smile can brighten your day; for me it was working.

CHAPTER 27

You will always come
back to Wales

I was told by a friend that once I had visited Wales,
I would always want to return, and he wasn't wrong.
There is just something mystical about the landscape,
almost like a magnetic pull. Running through Barmouth
and down to Abersoch, the coast line is constantly
changing. It's not like a holiday resort where everything
is about the beach, rather it's about the entire place; the
beach is just one attraction. The running was fantastic
and I had been helped massively by the weather. I had
hardly any rain for a good five day stretch which was
perfect and made everything better.

I worked out a way to help the pain in my legs; instead
of just running constantly on one side of the road, wherever possible I would zig-zig across the road, meaning
that my running was pushing off each foot rather than
the camber of the road constantly attacking one side
of me. It helped massively, and although it might have
looked strange to any oncoming traffic or pedestrian, it
meant that I was able to take the pressure off one side.

By this point of the run, I would be lying if I said I wasn't thinking about the finish line. If I'm honest, it was the only thing on my mind. In fact, it was constant. I would make lists of things that I wanted to do in my head:

1. Sit down for more than an hour.
2. Have a meal where I didn't think, "Has this got enough carbs in?"
3. Have a warm bath which is not followed or preceded by an ice bath.
4. Throw my running trainers in the bin.
5. Take Sara out.
6. Say about 50 million thank yous.
7. Start planning the next one.

Number 7 would probably shock most people, but by this time, I knew I would make it. My body had enough in me and I was managing pain much better than at any other time during the run. That was pretty good – it had only taken me 46 days to manage the pain! With so much time on my hands everyday, it was impossible to not think about another challenge. Could I run further? Could I run faster? I knew that I certainly could not fit many more miles into a day. The longest day had already been about 15 hours and any longer would have been a massive mistake. I thought about different disciplines and whether they would be possible. As I said right at the start, my main aim was to do something that people thought impossible, but also do something that no one else had done. That was the toughest part. Exploration of the Earth is pretty much done. I am not a big fan of flying and I don't think NASA will be knocking at my door anytime soon to go into space. It is my opinion that real people relate better to real life things, things that a normal person can do. As previously mentioned, I am no different than anyone else, in fact, I know there are millions of people who are much fitter than I am and there are certainly better runners. What I am is driven. I am driven to try and see exactly what I was put here for, and I believe it's to see just how much a body can take, whether that is mentally or physically.

CHAPTER 28

Almost home

I was nearly there. The buildings, the landscape, the accents – they all started to sound a lot more like home. The feeling of being nearly home was starting to excite me and also make me very nervous. I had been running for 2 months and I knew nothing major had changed, but I had changed. I had seen things and felt things that had changed me forever. I was nervous about what might be waiting for me in Skipton. Would there be anyone there to see come home or would it just be my Mum and a few friends who had joined me previously on the run? I hadn't seen my brother since Scotland and I knew that my body had changed quite a bit, so I wondered what they might say about that. There was so much to think about that the last few days kind of merged into one massive celebration and one massive sigh of relief.

The roads were much busier now I was back on English soil. I had moved away from the coast and was driving my run straight up the heart of England through Chester, Wigan and on towards Padiham. I would stay in Burnley on my last night, and this is where my 50 days would end. My fiftieth day was spent in Burnley having a few soft drinks and a meal with some friends. It was perfect. I could not have asked for anything more. My fifty-first day would be spent running 26.2 miles back to Skipton. I wanted this to be done in less than three hours which would be a good marathon pace. The reason it was done like this was so that anyone coming out to see me would not have to come out on a cold evening; instead, I would be finishing at 1.30pm on Skipton High Street.

Even when you know a place reasonably well, it is possible to get lost! I will never forget getting lost in Chester. I entered the underground pass which takes you from one side of a busy round about to another, you would think, with little worry. Five minutes passed as I ran around looking for the exit. When I finally did exit the underground, I was still on the same side. The only other time this had happened was when I did the same thing in Weymouth. What was going on? After some careful navigation, I finally emerged from the underground, thoroughly annoyed at myself, but when I think about it now, I imagine I looked pretty funny.

The stay in Burnley was fantastic; I laid in what was possibly my last ice bath on the run, knowing I had done it. I knew right then and there that I had done it. I had stared into the jaws of defeat, despair and pain, and I had won. I had beaten all the odds and I had proved them all wrong. There I was laying I a bath tub full of ice, legs still strapped from the days running, a brilliant cup of Yorkshire tea by my side. Nothing could take this smile; nothing could ever come close to this feeling.

CHAPTER 29

Home

I had done it; I was home and Skipton had never looked so good. I had smiled big, I had run hard and I was home. To anyone one reading this and thinking about their own challenge, whether it is big or small, anything is possible. People will always doubt you and tell you it can't be done, but these are just people who cannot do it themselves. Drive, determination, hard work and a massive smile are all you need. It's corny and it's not at all inspirational, but I have done it, and I'm just me, a 29 year old guy from Yorkshire who decided to go for a jog.

Running back into Skipton was one of the most surreal things I have ever done. My toots, donations and support was unbelievable! People lined the streets and were ready to cheer me into town as far as 8 miles out. What a fantastic feeling, to feel like what you have done has meant something to the people of your community. I would have been happy with my Mum and Dad, but what I got was so much more. I entered town from the north, heading up the bypass and had a agreed that I would do a loop through the park so some local school children could run with me. Once again, I had expected a handful of children to be there to run, not the sea of children I saw as I entered the park. It was mayhem; there were children and parents everywhere! My pace at this point was still a little bit high but I couldn't slow down, as adrenaline pumped through my veins and I knew I was nearly there. I had less than a mile to go. I had been to every point on the coast of mainland Britain and I was still running. 2,500 miles previously and 51 days earlier, I had set off from Blackpool with fear in my heart; I was now running into my home town with tears of joy streaming down my face. Pain was nothing – pain was a distant memory.

The streets were lined with people all donating into the buckets and if you were visiting Skipton for the day, it was impossible not to be drawn in, even for a second. I had pushed hard all morning to try and get under three hours for a marathon time. I finally crossed the finish line in three hours and ten minutes. I hadn't done the three hour limit, but I was happy. The crowd was brilliant! Everyone I wanted to be there was there, and they made coming home something I will never forget.

CHAPTER 30

Home and back to reality!

It was an amazing experience to sleep in my own bed, but one that was also a little alien to me. I woke up for the first time in 51 days and didn't have a plan. I didn't have to think, "What I am wearing today? Where is my route? What are the hills going to be like?" Even though everything was all over, my mind was still in over drive. There was still so much to do and so much to organise. It felt great to be in demand! I was being asked to open new centres, and to speak at dinners and galas where people wanted to come and talk to me and hear my story. All of this was why I chose to write a book about my journey. If I'm honest, I thought it would be easier to write the book, but it has proved one of the hardest things I have ever done!

I was given more advice once I had finished the run than I ever had when starting it! "Don't just stop!" they would say. "You have to keep moving," they added. In the end, you know what's best for your body. No one else giving this advice had run 50 miles, let alone done it 50 times over, so maybe, for the first time, I would listen to my body and my body was saying,"Stop!"

I had done damage to my body while I ran; there was not much doubt about that. The extent of the damage was something else entirely. I was given a full check up by the doctor and there were a few things that I was told I maybe could do just to help my body recover. Firstly, I write this from the comfort of a chair that has a reclining mechanism; this is great for being able to rest my legs and take the weight off my knees. I was told to ice my knees and my joints for the first few weeks to help the inflammation go down. My Achilles tendon in my right ankle had almost doubled in size. This tendon apparently moves up and down a sheath which protects it; mine was grating inside the sheath due to the swelling which made any movement of my toes very uncomfortable. When I was running, this would always subside during the day as my body warmed and I got use to the aches and pains. Now I wasn't running and I was going from sitting to standing to not doing a great deal at all, it burnt constantly and would often stop me dead in my tracks with a shooting pain. My right hip had taken the battering off a life time. Imagine having your right arm straight up in the air, and someone has hold of your hand and foot, and from there, someone else is kicking you in the hip every day for 12 hours. Eventually, you try and protect yourself by bending and trying to stop the pain. I had been doing this so long that the muscles and tendons around the hip were all inflamed and very tight. My hip flexors were so tight, along with my hamstrings, that they were like violin strings – one sudden movement and I expected to hear the twang of snapping muscles! My left knee had twisted so badly that there was a small stress fracture that had calcified and turned into hard bone. This is still here today and juts out of my knee just under the knee cap. The pain from this isn't so severe, until I catch it on something, or I bang the calcified bone by accident.

Much of the pain in my body I knew would heal, but where the run had affected me most was in my mind. I had been so focused for so long that I had missed the things that were important to me and important to those around me. It had affected the people I love and the people I hold dear to me more than ever. For that, for what I put you through, and probably continue to put you through, I am sorry.

Someone said to me recently while I joked about my next challenge, "Sam, don't you think it's time to grow up?" I believe that the day my imagination stops thinking about crazy challenges or thinking about what I might be able to do next, will be the day they put me in a box. Growing up certainly does not mean giving up on your dreams; it doesn't stop you pushing yourself to be the best version of yourself. No matter what life throws at me and the countless mistakes I make, I will always come back stronger, better and more determined not to make that same mistake.

I know that one day I will fail; I will fail a challenge that I have set myself. I fear that day, but I know it will happen. One day my body will say, "This is too much," but until that day, I will always push myself to the extreme. As my favourite film says, "Get busy living, or get busy dying."

CHAPTER *31*

The next challenge!

I have looked at hundreds of different challenges over the months since completing the run. I have been offered great opportunities to travel and be part of amazing teams with amazing people. The truth is, I still don't know what I am going to do.

My first challenge is to go from 11 stone 5 lbs and try and be my heaviest at 16 stone. I would like to see how much weight I could put on in a year. This for many of you might seem easy – just go and eat loads, but I want the weight to be clean. I want to add lean muscle, so it's functional muscle that I can move around easier. I think a great challenge would be to see if I can still move 16 stone around easy and try and do a similar endurance challenge, but at a heavier weight.

I have found that the hardest thing for me has been getting back into normal life. I sometimes see people looking at me now in the street wondering where they know me from, and it's a great feeling not only to be recognised, but to be asked about the run, what it did to me and how I made it.

CHAPTER 32

The Blog

I added the blog pages at the end just in case there were a few people that wanted to see the run through a diary version. I should warn you that I didn't get my laptop until after about a couple of weeks in, and when trying to update in the middle Scotland on a phone, it can get quite frustrating, hence, the reason why the earlier updates are very short. I do enjoy how they build and how more and more people started to like the pages; it really was a fantastic way to communicate with people. Something else to warn those die hard grammatical correctness people out there is that these blogs are the raw material taken straight from the blog and put on to a page. These are my exact feelings everyday for you. There is also a copy of the schedule that my run took and the places I set off from. I have added this just in case you ever feel like a challenge or a little jog for a couple of months.

Day	Date	Distance (miles)	From	To
1	6th April	50	Blackpool	Carnforth
2	7th April	100	Carnforth	Thwaite Flat
3	8th April	150	Thwaite Flat	Workington
4	9th April	200	Workington	Longtown
5	10th April	250	Longtown	Dalbeattie
6	11th April	300	Dalbeattie	Wigtown
7	12th April	350	Wigtown	Auchencrosh
8	13th April	400	Auchencrosh	Irvine
9	14th April	450	Irvine	Dumbarton
10	15th April	500	Dumbarton	Inveraray
11	16th April	550	Inveraray	Druimarbin
12	17th April	600	Druimarbin	Gorthleck
13	18th April	650	Gorthleck	Elgin
14	19th April	700	Elgin	Inverurie
15	20th April	750	Inverurie	Montrose
16	21st April	800	Montrose	Leven
17	22nd April	850	Leven	Edingburgh
18	23rd April	900	Edingburgh	Berwick On Tweed
19	24th April	950	Berwick On Tweed	Blyth
20	25th April	1000	Blyth	Middlesborough
21	26th April	1050	Middlesborough	Bridlington
22	27th April	1100	Bridlington	Immangham
23	28th April	1150	Immingham	Skegness
24	29th April	1200	Skegness	Kings Lynn
25	30th April	1250	Kings Lynn	Cromer

Day	Date	Distance (miles)	From	To
26	1st May	1300	Cromer	Lowestoft
27	2nd May	1350	Lowestoft	Ardleigh
28	3rd May	1400	Ardleigh	Tillbury (Gravesend)
29	4th May	1450	Tillbury (Gravesend)	Dover
30	5th May	1500	Dover	Westham
31	6th May	1550	Westham	Bognor Regis
32	7th May	1600	Bognor Regis	Christchurch
33	8th May	1650	Christchurch	Bridport
34	9th May	1700	Bridport	Newton Abbot
35	10th May	1750	Newton Abbot	Plymouth
36	11th May	1800	Plymouth	Penzance
37	12th May	1850	Penzance	Davidstow
38	13th May	1900	Davidstow	Barnstable
39	14th May	1950	Barnstable	Burnham on Sea
40	15th May	2000	Burnham on Sea	Caerphilly
41	16th May	2050	Caerphilly	Ammanford
42	17th May	2100	Ammanford	Tregaron
43	18th May	2150	Pembroke	Fishguard
44	19th May	2200	Fishguard	Aberystwyth
45	20th May	2250	Aberystwyth	Barmouth
46	21st May	2300	Bangor	Ruthin
47	22nd May	2350	Ruthin	Runcorn
48	23rd May	2400	Runcorn	Blackrod
49	24th May	2450	Blackrod	Padiham
50	25th May	2500	Padiham	Skipton RFC

Day 1.

First day done!! Just having a brew in Carnforth! Loved it today!! People actually handing money to me in the street!! Broken Britain my bum!! Come run with me for a day and you will see how great people in Britain are!!

Day 2.

Hurt today! Much more quiet roads. Tough climbs. Just carb loading now.

Day 3.

Day three done and dusted!! Much better day, better running, brilliant scenery, mum and dad turned up for a few miles and I get to have a bath!!

Day 4.

Losing three toenails! Ow. Rained all day!! Scotland here I come!!

Day 5.

New driver tom arrived. Had all seasons today. Running in hail is not pleasant!!

Day 6.

Run.....walk....crawl if u have to. That was the motto of today. Tough day. Amazing people all day donating and pipping support! Enough to keep anyone going!!

Day 7.

Second day in a row of pain in my knee. Had my medication advice from the great Jane Peggs hopefully that will do the trick! Been an awesome day up here, great weather, scenery and people. Need more likes on here!! Get sharing and reposting! Tom (driver) wants 400 by tomorrow (Friday I think) evening.

Day 8.

Both legs are taking a real beating at the moment. Driver tom has finished and Kate arrives tonight. Once again amazing scenery for running. Went along the electric brae today too!! Keep going everyone maybe 500 likes tonight!! Thank u for all the texts, tweets, likes and emails they are fantastic. Going to tackle Glasgow tomorrow!!

Day 9.

Painkillers, protein shakes and pma. A great chapter for my book and the only way of getting through a day!! Good running this morning, crisp spring sunshine and a few peeps from the passing traffic for motivation. The ice and ibuprofen routine is becoming very much a daily ritual. No video today I am afraid, logged myself outta you tube and can't remember my password! Tough climbs tomorrow up "rest and be thankful"!! Then up to Inveraray!! Brother arrives tomorrow for a little bit of running. Thanks for all the new likes!! Your challenge is to get us to 1000 likes by the time I get back to England next week!!!

Day 10.

A good day running round long loch, up rest and be thankful and on to Inveraray. Amazing view from the top of rest and be thankful. Next driver (Trev) my brother has arrived and ran with me this afternoon after Sara had left this morning. Meeting a guy this morning who gave a very generous donation but more importantly came with jelly babies was brilliant!! Really helped pick me up! Ice bath tonight was horrific! Keep the likes, texts, tweets, calls and donations coming.

Day 11.

Better day today. Legs feeling better, thanks mainly to jacqui parfitt an awesome physio in fort William! Ice bath was once again horrible but amusing for those that can hear me scream!!!! Trying to find things to keep my mind engaged while running is tough, started to learn Spanish and i quite often do the voice of the Geordie guy that does the voice over on big brother!! "day eleven" said in the Geordie accent! My brother has kept my spirits up by peeping the horn everytime I stop for a pee as well which he finds very amusing! Loch Ness tomorrow.

Day 12.

Much better day today. Ran hard and abit faster today, mainly just to keep warm as it was snowing this morning in fort William. Had to change clothes as I got soaking wet!! Legs are sore again but the ice baths are doing the job. Lovely running next to loch ness. Roads are pretty scary as there are massive logging trucks but hopefully tomorrow the roads should be a little more quiet. Thanks to all the new likes, please keep going with the shares and posts! Hopefully hit the 1000 mark by Friday!

Day 13.

Much better day today all round. Have worked out that it's better to go out hard and abit faster in the morning. Get through more miles before dinner then wind down gradually in the afternoon as starting again after dinner is always tough. Passed RAF Kinloss and Lossiemouth today which was awesome. The planes were so close today I think I could see the pilot!! Not good trying to look at them as I tend to drift in to the middle of the road!! The blue strapping sent by Jane Peggs has worked wonders for my knees, with very little pain today. It's now more about pain management, as the pain is always there. Heading more in land tomorrow so quite a few tough climbs to tackle. If every person that is a "new like" can share my page with all your friends and they do the same, in theory it should keep growing. Today my soundtrack was Adele first up followed by queens greatest hits then abit of learning Spanish!! Still not great at that though!!

Day 14.

Really tough day today. Went out this morning really hard and made good mileage but as the weather turned for the worse the climbs got harder and harder. Getting to lunch time was fine but then my ankle began to swell and it became so swollen I had to take my trainer off.

I strapped my ankle and ran as hard as I could but my pace was really down making every step this afternoon very painful. I have been quite lucky with the weather so far and was due a tough day. Hopefully tomorrow will be better. Unfortunately my headphones stopped working so I was not able to talk to people or listen to music so ended up talking to myself! I apologise if you saw me today as I was swearing at myself quite alot. Luckily my phone was working so I can see the messages and likes coming in. I know I say this every time but please keep sharing and posting my page!! As well as distance goals the "likes" goal of 1000 help keep me going.

Day 15.

Much much much better day. Got mad at myself for nearly giving up yesterday so got up early this morning and went out fast! Needed to do 57 miles today to catch up a couple from yesterday. Went hard and fast all day and felt great! The midafternoon dip in the sea really helped, I was able to get my muscles iced then get changed and crack on. I can safely say I have worked for every single pound of your donations today. Not only running but changing the chemical toilet in the van was not a highlight of my journey especially when the bottom came off and the contents went all over my foot!!! Mum was not a great help as she was laughing too hard to help me! Next highlight was running through Montrose where my mum (driver) said she would wait for me at the other side of the town so we did not hold up the traffic. 10 miles later I had still not seen my mum so I rang her. She was still sat reading the paper in a car park!!! I had just run up a massive hill with rain beating down!

Once again my mum was struggling to drive as she was laughing so hard when she caught me up. I have managed the pain in my ankle with heavy strapping and it seems to have done the trick. Thanks everyone for the jokes, texts, calls, tweets and facebook shares! Please keep them all coming!

Day 16.

What a great day! Rained for 4 hours this morning but nothing was stopping me today! Broken my day down now into 2 sets of 13 miles then 3 sets of 7 miles in the afternoon. I then just have a few miles to finish off the day! A highlight of today was running past St Andrews Golf Course and been joined by a random cyclist who made 13 miles seem very fast. The weather was much better this afternoon and it was great to be on the coast for the last 20 miles. It was great to hear my mum describe me as the duracell bunny! A kid was trying to give me a donation today while I was running so set off after me but gave over after about half a mile and just settled to handing the fiver to my mum in the van. If you are reading this, I am sorry I was listening to Bruce Springsteen and running quite fast to Born in the USA. Once again thanks for the many messages of support. To all the people that share and like this page I cannot thank you enough! Tomorrow we tackle Edingburgh! Should be interesting!

Day 17.

Another good day of running. Weather was perfect for running infact it was too hot!! I know that is hard to believe in Scotland but I had to put sun screen on!! I do (for those that dont know me) have the same skin tone as a polar bear, hence the sun screen. The Forth Bridge did nothng but reaffirm my tremendous fear of heights. There was not much running done across there as i wasnt able to let go of the railings!!! I was going to film the run across there for you but everytime I looked down I had to hold on! It was amazing to run through the streets of Edinburgh and passed Musselburgh racecourse. It was quite a change from the past week of running through forests and having mountains round me. I was back to running in civilisation. It was good to have people around me and to see other runners out on the pavements. Its a strange feeling to think i will be back in England tomorrow! I have loved running through Scotland, even during a bad day the scenary has been amazing. I have ended my day in a sleepy little town right on the seafront called Aberlady. Tomorrow night I will be writing to you from Berwick on Tweed in England!! Ok guys now for the serious bit! Lets get to 1000 likes tonight! If every single one of you share the page then we would make it!!! Lets do it!! Keep them coming!! Please keep all the messages and calls coming in and dont forget that if you text me please put your name on the text.

Day 18.

Happy St. Georges Day people! Back in England and it feels great to be back. Back to pain again today though. Started this morning in glorious sunshine and ran really well till about 2pm. After starting back out this afternoon I usually free up a little bit but today my knee would not loosen off. Thankfully I had already got the bulk of the running done. The weather has once again been amazing and I was able to run most of the day in just my skins. I was pushed hard today knowing that we had hit 1000 likes last night which is just fantastic. I have videoed my ice bath tonight for your amusement, but dont panic I keep my shorts on! I am now on the Easy Coast all the way down to Dover which is great and I will soon be back in Yorkshire as well. I will definitely miss Scotland. Scotland has been amazing and the people have all been fantastic. Today was another example when an elderly couple stopped what they were doing put their bags down and started applauding me while I ran past. Another lady stopped in front of me and donated £10 into the van. It made me wonder, that if I saw some mental guy running through town followed by a van what would I do... Probably think "what a nutter"! It was quite a humbling experience. As normal, thank you to everyone for the likes, shares, texts and tweets. While you guys share I will try and repair.

Day 19.

Sorry people but it's been a rubbish day today. Trying not to feel sorry for myself today. Went to the physio this afternoon once the pain had got to bad, he was an evil little buggar! Thought he was going to pull my leg off!! Have a strange hard lump on the front of my knee that has come from the way I run but its not something that will make me stop, will just be uncomfortable for a while. I have got company tomorrow and I canot wait to have someone run with me all day. Just some one to talk at me for a while. Ran to Holy Island this morning which was good as the tide was out. Would have been pretty scary had the tide been coming in I imagine!! Was worth the awful weather and the pain in my knee just for the view when we got there. Although today has been incredibly painful, Gayle Sharp text me this evening and made me remember the reason I am running. I am running for those that cant. Thank you Gayle. Having read the comments that many of you have written i think the new target should be 2,500 likes by the time I am finished. That would be one like for every mile! Lets see how we go. Hopefully tomorrow will be a better day.

Day 20.

What a great day! Weather this morning was good but was like a waterfall this afternoon!! Running in a monsson is not great put Tony "The Fridge" Morrison (Pictured below at the end of today) kept me going all day! Tony also was able to see just exactly how the run changes your views of people. A Hoody/Chav (apologies if you are now liking this page and it was you) approached us today just outside Sunderland and asked us "Is it you thats doing that run?", "yeah" I replied nervously. He then went on to say what an amazing challenge it was and as he left donated £10. Never judge a book by its cover, what a fantastic lad. Today I have run with Tony all day it has been great to have someone there telling me about why they love doing crazy challenges and there own reasons for wanting to run 50 miles. Its amazing the things you talk about over 50 miles! It was also fantastic to have my very own psycological profile done this morning from Gayle, Kirstie and Jo while running don a Dual Carriage way. One of the best questions ever.... Bush or Shaven

Haven???!!!! (Sorry if you are under age and reading that). My knee was good today with not too much discomfort which was massively due to having someone there to talk to so I didnt think about it all day. I step back in to Yorkshire tomorrow and cannot wait! Hopefully you have all seen the other update about texting Chris Moyles in the morning!! Lets really hammer it! The likes are fantastic and please keep them coming. I read all your comments every night, they are fantastic!

Day 21.

Tough day running. Got through some good mileage this morning coming down from Redcar to Scarborough. Was great to run along the beach and to see people from home. Nevermind about the Chris Moyles thing, I think Gayle Sharp has a new idea which is much better. Lets get the kids involved and try to inspire them for the future. I for one certainly like this idea better. Had to change clothes after about 30 minutes this morning as the rain belted down, almost like having a bucket of water thrown over me. In Filey tonight which is a lovely place. I am trying to upload a video i took of me running this morning up a monster climb. I have noticed that Whitby has a couple of very steep hills!!! They were not pleasant at all. A person called Joanne Stork posted this to me a couple of days ago and i listen to it every morning now. The first line of this rings true for me every day.

Day 22.

Ow ow ow ow ow ow ow ow! Toes are bad today and shin is hurting but with a tail wind most of the day the miles sailed on by. Today was a good day as people joined me for the run, especially the last section of the day which is always painful. Meeting me at the Humber Bridge and running through Barton and Barrow was great. Amazing sleepy little villages. Donations through the van window have been great today. I have made an awesome video today aswell, which has helped raise my spirits abit but will be late as i am off to eat my body weight in pizza! No messing about when it comes to food. 2 starters, 2 mains and 2 puddings! Even after 22 days I still love it when i talk to people on the street and you can see their reaction when I tell them what I am doing. The usual answer at the moment is bloody hell, i dont think i could do 50 yards! Weather today has been good and my milk bottle like tan is going well. A nice red line across my neck!! It feels pretty good knowing I am getting close to half way. Someone else has mentioned reading my book which is good it might mean that I will sell at least 4 copies of it! I did have a thought that I would walk into my mums and there just been 1000 copies stacked up just so i didnt feel bad! My mum is a legend! Hopefully she will like the video. Keep liking guys, keep sharing. Hopefully see some of you over the weekend.

Day 23.

As always seems to be the case a couple of ok/good days are followed by one very very bad day!! Had no sleep at all last night and a shocking day on the road. Wasnt able to concentrate on anything today. I have done alot of swearing at the top of voice knowing that the wind would not allow anyone to hear it! The wind has turned against me today and made every step a battle. I have also discovered that running and singing at the top of your lungs makes people look at you like you might be a touch crazy!! The songs I was singing would have also been quite strange for some... You're the Best Thing by Style Council, Kiss Me by Ed Sheeran, Neutron Star Collision by Muse and At Last by Etta James. All of these songs were screamed at the top of my lungs! Hoping anyone would hear them. Thankfully I remembered what Jane Peggs had told me "keep my best memories and lock them up tight and when things get really hard use those memories to get you through" . Thanks Jane. I listened to Tracy Chapman - Fast Car after this and it just made me smile even if was just five minutes. I am in "sunny" Skegness now and heading down to Kings Lynn tomorrow. Supposed to be one of the worst days of the year (weatherwise) tomorrow but hopefully my body will be better. It was commented last time that I should never feel sorry for myself and I dont, next time things get hard I will try to remember and just smile. At the end of pain is success.

Day. 24

What a bloody fantastic day!! It was amazing!! The weather can only have been described as torrential but even that was not stopping me today!! Joined by a hoard of people all day it was brilliant! With all the people running or cycling with me it made the day go really fast and even people at the end of the phone my my already big smile massive!!! Thank you, just for talking to me. As already mentioned the weather today has been awful so to clock a time of under four hours for my first marathon was great! One major amusement for me today was to have Matt Speres (A native of South Africa, a much warmer country than this) cycling next to me wearing nearly 40 layers of clothing one of which was a ski jacket!! Brilliant! I did mention to the guys that joined me today that I am actually getting nervous about writing my updates as my followers grow!! I should apologise now for my spelling and grammar! My younger brother (English Teacher) would probably not be to happy with it!! On the menu tonight was a Dominos Meal Deal for 4 with 2 puddings!! Carb Loading!! You What!! One of the guys who joined me today would like to get the likes over 1500 today! This is where you guys work hard! Lets get sharing! Onto Cromer tomorrow from a now annoyingly dry Kings Lynn!!

Day 25.

It feels great even to write that!! Everything from now is counting down. Continuing on from yesterdays good running today was also a good day! It always helps when the sun is out. First time in 25 days that I have been able to wear a vest when running and not have to have 6 layers, my beanie hat and gloves on!! Think I might even have a tan line! Although I ran well and was well fuelled my camper van was not, and ran out of fuel about 14 miles outside Cromer!! OOOOPPPPSSS! Luckily we were only half a mile from a garage. A quick top up and a trundle down to the petrol station and all was sorted! I was so glad it was just fuel running out as my mechanical expertise runs out at the windscreen wash stuff!!! I have been told a couple of lies while on my run. 1. Everything from Scotland South is down hill. Not true. 2. You do get use to ice baths. Again, not true. Tonight, was the worst ice bath yet, as while i was slowly lowering myself into the freezing water I slipped plunging my entire body very quickly into the ice cold water!! After gasping for breath and swearing at anything and everything in the bathroom, I managed to lay still. A highlight from today was passing another runner who was also wearing tights. He might think me a little odd but i couldnt stop staring at him! He was either very very blessed or he was hiding a torch! Today we got 90 toots and there were only 5 near misses!! Thats a pretty good day! Tonight instead of going for a number of likes lets try for a number of shares!! If each person can share this update then in theory the likes should go up!! Worth a shot!!

Day 26.

Today was supposed to be a good day, heading home, passed half way, counting down and generally good stuff. Unfortunately it didnt happen quite like that! The awful weather returned this morning and it was freezing, coupled with an unbelieveable pain in my ankle/knee/shin on my left leg the day has been an absolute battle. I have heard things described as blood, sweat and tears before. Today was that day. Heading out of Cromer the horn honking was good and the near misses minimal. After about 1.5 hours of running the rain was coming down so hard I couldnt raise my head to look forward due to the wind and rain so spent the majority of the morning staring down at the floor. Thank you to everyone for the peeps and honks, they always help. One person this morning was my highlight of today who has written to me on here, the smiles and cheers from the kids coming past this morning really kept me going. In Great Yarmouth tonight. Painkillers going down well. Dont panic, not to many. Been reading all your messages today and looking at all your shares just to try and keep me going. Thank you, every single one of you for liking, texting and sharing. For all you doubters, I am not stopping, I am on my way home, even if I crawl into Skipton I just want to see your faces. Before I go, Thank you to the Grove Hotel at Cromer who let me stay free of charge last night and gave me a fantastic meal. For anyone visiting the area, go there!! Well its that time again guys!! SHARE SHARE SHARE. As Gayle Sharp says EPIC RUN FEVER!!!

Day 27.

Day 28.

Better day today. Not quite free flowing but going better than yesterday, i suppose after 28 days I wont be free flowing! I woke up this morning to find out I was an Uncle again. Welcome to the world baby Wellock, all 8 pound 10 ounce of you! Puts my pain in perspective. Running towards London during rush hour was not a pleasant experience! The near miss to car horns ratio was a lot closer today! I am starting to feel like a cartoon character where the rain cloud just follows them round. Yes it rained, again. Just read that over the next few days there are flood warnings and the temps are going to drop again! Lovely jubbly. Just have to run quicker I reckon?? Managed to get right round past Gravesend and into to Whitstable today which is awesome as it means tomorrow should be much better. The roads should be quiter meaning I can get a better stride pattern. I could feel the tension in my shoulders today as I ran. One thing that kept me going today was a message from a follower on here telling me of a friend who has just lost both legs but was recieving great care at Camp Bastion. That's why I am running. Tomorrow I will see the White Cliffs of Dover for the first time ever, really looking forward to it. I always want to try and write something motivational to finish off, but I suppose the best thing I can put is that I have inspired a 40 year old mother of 2 to enter a marathon. That is enough for me. As always, share share share! Lets try 2000 likes? I think you have it in you!!

Day. 29

3 weeks to go!! Today has been a great day! If you are eating your tea I apologise for the next bit. I have had a really bad stomach today so my pace has been pretty good, between toilets!! Perfect running weather, no head wind, not raining but not to hot. Blasted out of the blocks today heading East towards Hernes Bay then moved southwards towards Canterbury. It was great to have dinner in a town called Sandwich. I am a geek, so it was ace to be able to have a sandwich in Sandwich (well i thought it was funny). Maybe thats what happens after 29 days of running. Got into Dover late afternoon running along the costal paths until the cliffs came into view. It was great to stand and look at them for a while. I ran along an ancient road today which was great. My only fear at the moment is not that I wont finish but I will fall down a pothole or slip off a pavement! I concentrate so hard on where I put my feet, much more

than i was at the start. I got 94 honks and only 4 near misses today so a pretty good ratio. Tomorrow I start along the South Coast. I have also had one of the best ever donations - A Sheep and Two Lambs!! Selling tomorrow at Gisburn Auction with all proceeds going to Epic Run! Playlist today was We Are Young - Fun, Unbelievable - EMF and Dominick the Donkey - Lou Monte (yes i know thats a xmas song). Bit of a Mayday call now! I need a driver for Monday afternoon, Tuesday all day and Wednesday morning if anyone is free or knows someone who might be free on the South Coast. Near Bridport Area. I should also mention that I got an email from Dean Karnezes last night. This guy is the Ultra Running equivilant of David Beckham! It was ace! Hope everyone has a good Bank Holiday. If you see me out give me a toot! If not a text, share or like are equally as awesome.

Day 30.

Another day done and dusted. The miles shot by this morning. It was great to meet some people along the way today. Had a little welcoming party this morning just outside Folkestone which really made my morning. Wind at my back all day, running on the sea wall and only a couple of tough climbs made today a flipping good day. Topping off a great day running was hearing that Gisburn Auction raised £545 today!! Thank you to all who were involved there. Tomorrow I run from BexHill to Bognor Regis, heading through Eastbourne and Brighton, hoping for a similar day. Epic Run Fever certainly seems to be going international now which is just awesome. Thank you to all the new likers and sharers. Playlist today was the Rocky 3 and 4 soundtrack. Eye of the Tiger = Brilliant. Also listened to Nessum Dorma (which might be quite sad but sends chills down my spine every time) and also the entire Avenue Q soundtrack which is again quite sad but very funny! I cant believe how well the miles went today, such a great day. I know for most this must get boring but once again like like like share share share. If you are running tomorrow, good luck, I hope like today was for me that the wind is at your back the whole day.

Day 31.

Another good day along the South Coast. Great to see some familiar faces this morning just outside Bexhill and then again this afternoon in Brighton. It was strange to run in Brighton with so many people on the road and on the pavements in comparison to Scotland when i would only see two people in the entire day! Eastbourne was really good but my god there was a climb coming out of there and round to Beachy Head. It was great running again with the wind at my back. The people down here have been great with some stopping and applauding while I ran past which was a great feeling. Its Bognor Regis tonight and HMS Dragon tomorrow which should be great then onto Christchurch. Got 54 Honks and 4 near misses today. Playlist today included Kasabian - Underdog (Played very loud), Westlife - You Raise Me Up (Yes I am that cool) and Up Around the Bend - Creedance Clearwater Revival. The problem with having alot of people around you is that they look at you a touch strange when you are singing while you run along the promenade in Brighton! Someone mentioned today, how strange it was to be in a large group of people and them not knowing where i have run from! They just think i am another runner, out for a Sunday afternoon jog along the beach. Little do they know! Here is the challenge, 2000 likes tonight?? Not a massive ask I don't think?? Lets GO GO GO!LIKE LIKE LIKE!!

Day 32.

Day 32...... I think? What a day. We cannot still be in a state of drought!! I was soaked all day! I do weirdly enjoy running in the rain. Massive thanks to Sara for driving the past week and to my emergancy drivers this afternoon who were drafted in at the last minute. Thank you to you all. Visited HMS Dragon this morning in Portsmouth, this is the Navys newest member of the fleet! Met some great servicemen and women on there and I got to sit in the captains chair! Stopping in Waterlooville tonight having some great food and hospitality, once again thank you to everyone who made this possible. Quite enjoying the South Coast, good donations, good people think we might have it wrong up North?? Havent met anyone who doesnt want to talk to me!! Still amazed at peoples generosity everyday, really glad my drivers get to see it. Book is coming along well, done a really good chunk of it today. Heading into Bridport tomorrow, back on the coast after a bit of the New Forest. Cant believe we have got to 2000 likes! Just amazing! Hello to all the new likes! Keep it going everyone! I'll keep running if you keep liking! Really feel like I am on the countdown now. I have been told that there might be some decent climbs tomorrow so will see how I go! Hoping for some better weather!

Day 33.

Its all over........... ha ha ha only joking but Epic Run nearly came to an unexpected end this morning when I was stuck in a bedroom! With the help of some lovely neighbours I got out and hit the road hard. Running through the New Forest and into Christchurch. From Christchurch I met up with my new driver and away I went. Down Bournemouth beach and onto Wareham. Today was warm and sunny with most of the running done in just a vest and running tights. Having never really spent any time in this part of the UK I can honestly say it is amazing. Some tough climbs but they are always worth it when you get to the top. Tonight I am stopping at The Bull Hotel in Bridport for free!! Many thanks for this, it is an amzing place and they even had the local paper here to interview me when I arrived. Not loving photo shoots at the moment as I look like Tom Hanks in Castaway. For those that have not seen it, he has a big beard! I should point out at some point that 50 miles still hurts! I just dont want to come on here and moan to you guys. If you are wondering about the pain.... here goes.... My left ankle is swollen and is iced every night, my right hip hurts with the constant thud of the road, an old break in my foot is now a massive lump and rubs hard against the top of my trainer, my left knee is twisting due to the cambre of the road making a small bone in the front pull hard against the tendon, my elbows ache constantly, my right knee burns at the slightest undulation in the road, I have one toe nail left on my left foot and my right achillies has swollen twice the size it should be and grates when i move. Other places are sore but I know children read this and so does my mum. Lets just say, one day I wore the wrong boxers!!

Day 34.

Today has been a monumentally tough day. Climb after climb after climb coupled with rain all day has made today long and miserable. Three of the climbs today had a gradient of 25%. The only problem with the climbs is that the down hill is equally as steep and hurts alot. Your messages have kept me going today. A message came through tonight at the end of my day saying they had passed me yesterday and they couldnt believe I was still smiling. Think thats the one thing I will remember from this, when everything hurts and your body is screaming to stop, just smile and plod on. Had to go up a size of trainer on my left foot due to the swelling but it was much more comfortable after the change. In Newton Abbott tonight heading towards Plymouth tomorrow. One highlight from today was running through the town of Beer, unfortuately I didnt have a beer in Beer. Sorry for the short update tonight. Shattered just doesnt cover it.

Day 35.

That was a lot of rain!! Might as well swim. Got changed 6 times today. Not good wifi so having to update from my phone. The head winds and rain were brutal today trying to beat me backwards. Got some great support today from car horns! Free hotel as well which is great! Feeling better today, everything hurts but smiling through the wind and rain just feels like another battle won. Only two more days on the south coast then for the first time I am heading north. That's right kids "the running man" is running home. I have a new website as well which is great!! Good pics and abit more info for people. Hello to every new liker and to the faithful out there, running hard and running home. Lands end tomorrow!!

Day 36.

Flipping great day! Weather was amazing all day which resulted in better running. Had great support from the get go this morning, people donating, tooting, waving and clapping. Been on the radio twice today too! Even had a dip in the sea which was so much better than the last time I did it in Scotland! Met up with some friends today who came armed with calories in the shape of a "medium" Cornish pasty. There was nothing medium about that bad boy! Think it could have sunk a ship! Awesome calories though. For the people asking about the beard, I am afraid it got the chop today. This is one occasion where forest gump beats me, how people manage to run or for that matter do anything with a full beard is baffling! Nearly itched my face off today. I am now going to ask something I didn't want to do all the way on this challenge. Your support for me and help for heroes has been outstanding and I hate asking. I am now starting to struggle with refuelling my support vehicle. This journey has been self funded apart from a few very kind donations and sponsors. If there is anyone out there who can help with a donation towards fuel or food please contact me on here or the contact form off my website or even a text. It would be so much appreciated! I have had to update off my phone again and I sometimes miss words or the predictive text decides what to put. If that has been the case I am sorry. Heading north tomorrow people! Cannot wait to take those steps northwards heading up through st Ives and Newquay should be good. Think I my new strap line might be "smiling big, running hard and running home".

Day 37.

Running in the sun. After the battering of the rain earlier in the week, today was a case of managing fluid intake. This morning my body knew that I had not taken enough on. Salt lined my hat from yesterdays sweat which is never a good sign. It seems a difficult balancing act, taking on enough liquid so I dont cramp but also not having so much that I get stomach ache. On a massive plus side I AM HEADING NORTH!! It is a great feeling to have turned the corner. I have now been as far North, South, East and West that I am going! At about 09.30 this morning I stood at Lands End and looked out. It was quite a strange feeling to be stood at the start/finish line of the Lands End to John O Groats challenge. I wondered how many tears had been shed on that line, how many welcome back parties had been thrown and how many people had stumbled over the line thinking "never again". The land is stunning down here it really is a privelage to run these roads. It was made a little easier today after shaving the beard. I was contemplating keeping the tash but couldnt look in the mirror without laughing...so off it went. A massive thank you to everyone who has donated funds to keep Epic Run going, it really was overwhelming. Although feeling very tired and drained, I have smiled alot today due to your generosity. Thanks again. I have loved people repeating my strap line and now i think i will sign off on it. Smiling big, Running hard and running home.

Day 38.

A cracking day on the road. The sun has been shining all day and even had a bit of topless running later this afternoon. The camper van did look like a mobile clothes horse for the majority of the day as I tried to dry my clothes! Rain seems like a distant memory now...It was great running weather today, breeze at my back, sun shining all the way along the coast. Got away well this morning and did a strong 17 mile block to start the day. Managed to get some of the food donated in St Ives down me and pushed hard, right through the afternoon. It was great. For a change of scenary think I might come away from the coast and run through Exmoor Forest tomorrow which should be good. Hitting Wales on Tuesday which i am really looking forward too. Every climb I hit today was worth it for the amazing views at the top. We passed through a small town called Boscastle today and got clap from some people sitting on a bench, it was a great feeling. I am sure they knew the massive decent into the town and the massive accent out again. Another driver arrives tonight to join the run. I am trying to upload the video of me running in the rain from the other day with one from today so you can see the contrast in weather. Hope you have seen the picture of the worlds sweatiest hat! I keep threatening my driver with putting the salt on his dinner while he is not looking!! If anyone is wanting to run a few miles just use the contact form on my website www.epic-run.co.uk Even if you are just bored I will always try and answer if I have service. I really look forward to getting in at night and looking at this page, your comments always make me smile and give me great motivation for the next day. Smiling Big, running hard and running home.

Day 39.

A good day running with the Army boys. It always makes the miles go well when you have someone to talk to. Starting off with two this morning but one stayed with me for a full marathon which was awesome, especially when he was running in Army Boots and combat trousers! Massive respect. Was abit damp this morning but it helped to cool the sun burn down from yesterday. Came out hot again this afternoon which was not to great as I went up a 25% hill for 2.5 miles. The sweat poured. If you are wondering what its like, the gym treadmills usually go to 15%. So try do that for 2.5 miles and see how much you sweat! or maybe do 35 miles first then try! Really enjoyed today. Pain was not too bad, the views were stunning coming through and out of Lynmouth. I hit the record for toots today aswell with a whopping 121!! Well done Devon. Was once again a great and humbling experience for me to receive donations on the road and really made me happy that the Army boys got to see it as well so they know how much they been to all of us. Should hopefully get into Wales tomorrow which I am really looking forward to. Lets try and get the likes up for the Army Boys today and for my new driver!! Lets show them what Facebook power can do!! SHARE people!! Like Like Like. Smiling big, running hard and running home!

Day 40.

A pretty good day all round. Made it to Wales!! Had to sellotape a pan on my head for a while down the A39. Got plenty of toots and a couple funny looks but never mind. Came up the west coast with plenty of support it was brilliant. Great day for running with the sun out and a slight tail wind. Would not recommend trying to run through Bristol and onto the Severn Bridge its quite busy to be honest! Heading onto South Wales tomorrow through Swansea. Never been down here before so should be good. After the climbs of late yestyerday my body has been screaming for me to stop today. Hamstrings and knees didnt feel like they had loosened all day. The ice bath was once again awful but actually felt the benefits of it tonight. Left it running abit long tonight though.... thought they were going to evacuate the restaurant downstairs! oooppss. Men do not multi task!! Do one thing, and do it well! Cannot believe i have run 2000 miles! Single figure countdown tomorrow. The texts and donations have been great today! Thank you. Please keep the likes coming and remember your challenge is to get to 2500 likes by May 26th. Smiling big, running hard and running home.

Day 41.

Actually feels good to write that today. Its been another great day of running. Had some company coming out of Cardiff and through Barry this morning which always help the miles go past. I am happy that even after 40 days of running I still managed to get a Three hour and 40 minute marathon time. I love that John Bishop has shared the page! Thanks to everyone who made this possible, and thank you John. I have just been reading the comments on his page with most people think its not possible. Well, come and find me. I am running along the South Coast of Wales. I entered Wales a little nervous, never sure how the people would react to a man running down the streets in tights followed closely by a campervan! I can safely say the people of Wales are awesome! They now lead the car honking league with a massive 139 honks today! Also got some great donations along the way. It was great to run with my top off for a while and get some sun on my milk bottle complexion! Factor 300 tomorrow I think. Managed to break another running partner today. His "runners knee" played up after 16 miles! I have really enjoyed today, even getting lost in Barry and having to use the dreaded chemical toilet (sorry if your having your tea). Nothing could stop me today! Please keep sharing this page! We are close to the 2500 mark. As always, smiling big, running hard and running home.

Day 42.

Had some great company again this morning, and he managed to achieve his goal of a marathon. Unfortunately I had another one still too go! Some really tough climbs today but still loving Wales. Lovely little beaches and winding country roads just help the miles tick by. Had a lovely stay at the Stradey Park Hotel in Llanelli last night and would recommend to anyone. Was up and out this morning and straight into 9 minute miles. I dont think my running partner had the same enthusiam for hills that I have, it tends to be the climbs that breaks people, but a great run with him all the same. Had some running repairs done on the van today, nothing abit of electrical tape couldnt fix! Come on Herbie only 8 more days! Hopefully you all saw John Bishops share of my page last night. What a flipping legend! A massive thank you to him for the support, it is very much appreciated. So much so I listened to his sunshine tour on my ipod today! You always look a bit of a nutter when howling with laughter and running up a killer climb. I have revised my running plan a bit as when i set off I did compansate for injury and illness, luckily this has not happened. So I have not filled those days with abit more running in Wales and also to try and get near John Bishop in Runcorn. Body wise the last couple have days have hurt! But with Bish sharing the page its given me a big push.

Day 43.

I dont know whether it was me getting complacent or over confident but today i was brought back down to Earth with a massive and amazingly painful bang! The miles still went by like normal but every step was met with a screaming pain through my left shin, right knee and right hip. The pain got so much it was making me feel sick. The pain has helped remind me that there is still some hard work to go! In Fishguard tonight heading to Aberystwyth tomorrow. Ran through St Davids today which is Britains smallest city which was cool and also through a village called Square and Compass which i think is an awesome name for a village. I am still loving Wales. Today made me dread seeing certain road signs. Downhill 12% = Pain. Uphill 12% = Pain. Blind Summit = Pain. Castle = Pain. Anytime you see a sign for a castle you know there is a reason why its still standing, and it is usually because the enemy could not be bothered going up the massive hill it is built on! Once again Wales was kind with car honks and the weather was on my side aswell with just a light shower later this afternoon. Aside from running I had the worst experience ever!!! I felt something moving in my tights this afternoon after 35 miles of running.... Pulling my tights off rapidly there was a huge spider moving down my leg!!!! Yes I am scared of them! No, I have no idea how long it had been in there or more disturbingly where it had come from!!! I am hoping it has no friends! Smiling big, running hard and running home.

Day 44.

Not the toughest day on the trip so far but well up there. Left shin is pulling hard on every climb and right knee and hip grate on every decent. Went to buy painkillers this morning and they only let me have 2 packs!! Might last till tomorrow?? Wales still throws some challenges my way every now and again but also shows some great scenary and amazing generosity. Not only is my body hurting but the chemical toilet was in full use as well. Support vehicle evacuated rapidly! A 6'3 man should not have to manouvre himself on to a toilet that is about 30cm tall! Its is not a good look!! Its always good to have someone run with you and even better when they are a good mate that never shuts up!! Best line ever today.... We were both answering the call of nature and he turns to me and says "they come in medium and large you know"!! Actually couldnt keep peeing as I was laughing so much. One thing I have really started to like is meeting people that have driven past us on the road and then stopped further up the road. They stop and chat and nearly always donate. One particular guy emptied all the change he had in his Landrover. Its amazing. Cannot believe that this time next week I will be back home. Have really enjoyed Tiffin and Lemon Drizzle cake today! Lots of calories! Up to Barmouth tomorrow. Smiling big, running hard and running home.

Day 45.

Another glorious day in sunny Wales, i think the locals would describe it as lush!!It has been a pretty good day, legs loosened off quite fast and was straight into my stride. It was good to have company today as many of the stetches were quite isolated coming up the coast. We stopped for dinner at a small town in a cafe that was certainly a "local place for local people". I do generally get funny looks when i am just wearing my running tights and a vest but today the stares were more like the ones I have seen in horror films. It never ends well for the innocent tourist! Moving rapidly after dinner I once again hit my stride and headed along the costal roads through Aberdyfi and into the gorgeous seaside town of Barmouth. The landscape here is hard to describe it is so amazing, with rolling green hills all the way down to the sea. I love looking out to sea at one side and at the other fields and hills as far as you can see. Tomorrow might be tougher as we enter Snowdonia National Park but hopefully not all the climbs will be killers! Took some good photos today especially one on top of the support vehicle. I was trying to look like I was surfing but even 10 feet up my fear of heights stops me from moving! Well done to all that took part in the Race for Life today hope you raised loads! Thanks for all the texts, shares and likes! I am sure I will need them all when i hit the climbs tomorrow. Smiling big, running hard and running home.

Day 46.

Today has been the first day where I have thought about the finish. I thought about getting home and what I am going to do on Sunday. Sitting down is pretty high on the "To Do List". Pain is now a constant part of my life, it is just all about pain management. I can manage the pain in my shin and i can manage the pain in my right knee but my right hip is something else entirely. Fortunately I have worked a way round this, when this pain comes on I run in Zig Zags down the road for a while, moving my weight from one foot to the other. I just look a little bit strange. Stopped in Menai Bridge tonight after running from Barmouth this morning. The roads were great for running, nice and wide. Ran down to Abersoch where I had dinner then across the Lleyn Peninsula and up through Caernarfon to Bangor. The sun has been shining all day and hopefully i will be bringing this weather back with me. I will definitely not miss shaving my legs after the run!! How people do this all the time is beyond me!! I think Stevie Wonder would do a better job! I have even had my milk bottle legs out today, first time I have worn shorts on the trip! Think there were more near misses after I put them on, as I dazzled people with my amazing white legs!! Some one suggested we aim for 3000 likes tonight! We havent done this in a while so lets give it a try!! Share share share like like like!! Smiling big, running hard and running home!

Day 47.

Its been a pretty good day today. Getting out of Bangor this morning after spending sometime at "The Unit" http://www.cgmfitness.co.uk/ which was awesome! Love looking at the way people train. Especially love meeting like minded people. Favourite line "train insane or stay the same". This run is hopefully insane enough! Pushed really hard for the rest of the day as just been back in a gym gave me motivation to kick my own ass up a gear. Feeling great now. Was strange to move away from the coast and begin the climb into England and back towards home. Some truly brutal hills today but as I have mentioned before I do enjoy the challenge of a hill. The best thing about Wales is the reward when you reach the top. The weather has really helped in this last week, the sun beaming down makes everything a bit easier. Had some great news about people covering the run but dont want to give too much away just yet but hopefully the run will be going national!! Well done and thank you to everyone who has made that possible. I arrived in the beautiful town of Ruthin this afternoon and I am staying at the gorgeous www.sirjohntrevorhouse.co.uk its awesome! Thank you to George at Bathingbeauty for my Osteopath help tonight. Might mean my hip will make it home!! Tomorrow I will step foot on English soil again, and continue my move up England towards Skipton High Street. I have a strange feeling of sadness, excitement and nervousness about getting home. The run has taken over everything and now it is coming to an end. I wanted to ask this last night?? What is the best song to have that motivates you?? Smiling big, running hard and running home.

Day 48.

Miles and miles of happy running. A great day returning onto English soil for the last time on this trip! What a great feeling. The sun was shining, people are smiling and the landscape is starting to look alot more like home. Setting out early this morning there is a huge climb out of Ruthin towards Mold but once that was conquered it was plain sailing all the way through Chester and up in to Runcorn later this afternoon. I love Chester, it felt great to be running on those old roads, looking at all the amazing buildings in the city. I think throughout the run my navigation has got much better, today I baffled even myself. Running through Chester there are a number of subways which help you cross busy roads. I somehow managed to go down one set of stairs spent five minutes underground and came up at the exact point which I had started! I still have no idea how I managed this. After a couple of minutes swearing at myself for my own stupidity I managed to cross the subway and emerge successfully at the other side. Fluid intake was once again a priority today, its getting tougher and tougher to take on enough as it makes me feel more and more sick. Yesterday I was nervous and a little sad about finishing but today I am just excited. I know my legs need to stop. Plus I want to start planning the next thing, ha ha ha ha. Thinking America?? Thanks to all who gave me ideas for my playlist. Today was Foo Fighters, James, Queen, ACDC, Quo, Limp Bizkit, Nirvana, Europe and some random songs like Jeruselam and You'll Never Walk Alone (Just for John Bishop). Tomorrow we continue Northup to Black Rod. Keep sharing guys lets get to 3000! If you want an Epic Run T Shirt they are £10. Just text me or send me a message on here or on the website contact form and I will sort them out for you! Smiling big, running hard and running home.

Day 49.

I have worked out that to beat the heat you need to start early hence the reason i can update earlier. Running early is great, really fresh and most of the world is still asleep. Went well again today but as the sun burnt through the pace slowed. Sweat poured from my cap, so much so that as i looked forward it looked like rain! The contrast in landscape is amazing. Not so long ago I was in beautiful St Ives, today I was in the not so gorgeous St Helens (apologies if you live there or come from there). It tells you alot about a place by how many times you stop to get dog poo out of your trainer!! Lovely. As I have said many times while on the run it has always been the local people and their support that pushes me on. Today was no different. A bloke, who can only be described as a chav, stopped at the side of the road, socks tucked firmly into his track suit bottoms, shirtless, began clapping and shouting "go on Sam!". At first I was a little concerned with how he knew my name, then I remembered it is plastered all over the van!! I smiled, gave him a thumbs up and pressed on to Wigan. As the day wore on I could feel my stomach cramping, the amount I was sweating was not been replaced fast enough. It is something I am really struggling with. Nearly there now though. Everyone else might be counting down the miles, for me, its two more ice baths to endure! Smiling big, running hard and running home.

Day 50.

Day 50. Almost home.... cooked again by the belting sunshine! Currently sat with friends having my last meal on the run! Please go and look at the story on the daily mail website and comment on the story. It will push the story! If I could thank everyone of you individually for the support you have given me over the last 50 days I would. Thank you from the bottom of my heart. I hope I have inspired and motivated you to get your trainers on and do something. Tomorrow I am looking to run my last 26.2 miles into Skipton in less than three hours. I will be heading into Skipton via Colne/Foulridge/Earby/Thornton and into Skipton via Grassington Road then turning Right past Tesco and then back up Coach Street turning left to the top of Aireville Park then back down the park with hopefully a load of kids and down to the rugby club. I am looking to hit the high street about 13.00. It should take about 10 minutes to get through town and down the park. Today has been a good day. Pain is still constant but now it subsides knowing that I am going to be home soon. I called in to Padiham Primary School today to an overwhelming scene. It was amazing! All the kids waving Help for Heroes Banners! It nearly broke me into tears. Think I might be wearing sunglasses tomorrow. Thanks to Stray FM for following me on my entire journey you have been great. I will keep updating when I have finish and hopefully I can get a book deal and tell you all about my run. I cannot wait to see you all tomorrow. T Shirts have pretty much sold out, if you still want one it will be after the weekend now. Thank you once again. As always.... Smiling big, running hard and running home.

Day 51.

Wow wow wow wow. What a flipping day!! The most amazing reception into Skipton. Thank you to every single person that made the welcome home so great!! Sorry for not speaking to you all but I think I would have broken down if I had made a speech. I will hopefully try and thank you all in the book! I am truly overwhelmed by the welcome today. Please look at some of the photos if you were not there. I will try get some videos uploaded at some point. I am really struggling with words tonight I just want to keep writing thank you!! If you want me to come and talk at your kids school I really would love to or any other group. If you want to come and train with me please contact me either on facebook or through the website. I promise it wont be just miles of running!! Back to the gym tomorrow and try and get some muscle back on. Just a massive thank you to everyone that made today possible. Please look out for me on BBC Look North on Monday dinner time. Hopefully going to be in the Sun next week aswell. Massive smile, massive run and home at last. Thanks.

Lightning Source UK Ltd.
Milton Keynes UK
UKOW05f2017090813

215091UK00001B/2/P